PLANTS & GARDENS

BROOKLYN BOTANIC GARDEN RECORD

THE
ENVIRONMENTAL
GARDENER

1992

Brooklyn Botanic Garden

STAFF FOR THIS EDITION:

JANET MARINELLI, EDITOR

BARBARA B. PESCH, DIRECTOR OF PUBLICATIONS

AND THE EDITORIAL COMMITTEE OF THE BROOKLYN BOTANIC GARDEN

BEKKA LINDSTROM, ART DIRECTOR

JUDITH D. ZUK, PRESIDENT, BROOKLYN BOTANIC GARDEN

ELIZABETH SCHOLTZ, DIRECTOR EMERITUS, BROOKLYN BOTANIC GARDEN

STEPHEN K-M. TIM, VICE PRESIDENT, SCIENCE & PUBLICATIONS

FRONT COVER: Sally Rasberry cuts flowers from a California garden
that is as lush as it is water thrifty. PHOTOGRAPH BY ROBERT KOURIK
BACK COVER: Pale purple coneflower, *Echinacea pallida*, one of scores of native wildflowers
that can be grown in a prairie garden. PHOTOGRAPH BY PATRICIA ARMSTRONG

Plants & Gardens, Brooklyn Botanic Garden Record (ISSN 0362-5850) is published quarterly at 1000 Washington Ave., Brooklyn, N.Y. 11225, by the **Brooklyn Botanic Garden, Inc.** Second-class-postage paid at Brooklyn, N.Y., and at additional mailing offices. Subscription included in Botanic Garden membership dues ($25.00) per year).

ISBN # 0-945352-70-0

PLANTS & GARDENS

BROOKLYN BOTANIC GARDEN RECORD

THE ENVIRONMENTAL GARDENER

VOL. 48, NO. 1, SPRING 1992

HANDBOOK #130

FOREWORD

Environmental gardening wasn't invented in the 1960s along with love beads and granola. As early as 1625, Francis Bacon declared that every garden should include "a heath or wilderness." It was one of the first recorded calls for more natural landscapes. The gardens of Bacon's day were formal spreads with knotted hedges and perfect symmetry. He described his new ideal, by contrast, as "nature imitated and tactfully adorned."

"Nature tactfully adorned" — statuesque trees on a sweep of green lawn — is as good a description as any of the typical American garden. This kind of manicured woodland was state-of-the-art natural gardening in the 17th century. But it's nature much too tactfully adorned for an age whose natural verdure is being stripped bare.

ABOVE: Purple prairie clover, *Dalea purpurea,* photographed in a prairie garden designed by Patricia Armstrong.

Our gardens have other environmental problems. Leaves, lawn clippings and other yard "wastes" account for nearly one-fifth of what ends up in overflowing landfills. More pesticide is used in home gardens than on agricultural lands. Home gardens suck up as much as 50 percent of domestic water.

So how do you create a garden that's both beautifully designed and environmentally sound? In a nutshell, you work with nature, not against it.

One way to work with nature is to create a zone of natural landscape in your yard. While wildernesses around the world continue to shrink, impoverishing the biological diversity of the planet, garden acreage is growing. Home gardens have a potential as ecological sanctuaries that's just beginning to be explored. In this handbook, pioneer natural landscapers explain how they create gardens that celebrate biological diversity and bioregional style — and how you can, too. Natural landscapers look to nature for broad patterns and a plant palette. They don't just use a native plant or two but rather recreate entire native plant communities or significant parts of them — whether oak forest in New York, tropical hammock in Miami or California coastal chaparral. What their diverse gardens have in common is they're designed to enhance surrounding native vegetation or, in areas where the local flora is long gone, restore what once flourished. And because they work with nature, not against it, they require much less coddling than their more cultured counterparts.

Does this mean that formal herb gardens and English-style herbaceous borders must be relegated to the dustbins of horticultural history? Not at all. That's where xeriscaping, the new name for common-sense gardening, comes in. One of the basic principles of xeriscaping is that you should select plants for your knot garden or perennial border which are suited to your climate — plants which won't require massive infusions of precious water.

No matter what the style, an environmental garden also works with the natural cycle of decay and renewal. In nature, nutrients absorbed by plants are returned to the soil in the form of fallen leaves, wild animal manures and other natural "refuse." It makes little sense to send leaves and lawn clippings to an overburdened landfill then scoot over to the garden center for peat moss and fertilizer when you can recycle yard "wastes" in your own backyard and nurture the natural processes of soil fertility.

By the same token, environmental pest control (so-called integrated pest management) begins with good garden design, selection of disease-resistant plants and an understanding of the interaction of pests and beneficial insects. Environmental gardeners work with the entire backyard ecosystem — not just the plants.

Despite its sometimes hifalutin terminology, environmental gardening is really simple common sense. Alas, terms like "xeriscaping" and "integrated pest management" are guaranteed to make even the most devoted gardener's eyes glaze over; I'm convinced they're a big reason why environmental gardening is not well understood or widely practiced. (Can you come up with catchier terms? Send your suggestions to me at BBG, 1000 Washington Ave., Brooklyn, NY 11225.)

In the pages that follow, gardening experts across the country cut through the jargon. Their articles are full of roll-up-your-sleeves practical advice on what you can do in your garden, day to day, to make a difference.

JANET MARINELLI
EDITOR

THE LAZY GARDENER'S GUIDE TO

RECYCLING YARD WASTE

BY ROBERT KOURIK

Not long ago, composting was considered the quaint hobby of horticultural eccentrics who wore rumpled flannel shirts and preached the gospel of organic gardening. In those days, composting had an aura of sacredness. I should know — I started composting in the mid-1970s with a passion that bordered on religious fervor. Compost gurus like myself rapidly decomposed garden wastes in what was variously called an "aerobic," "active," or "hot" compost pile. These piles reached internal temperatures of 130 to 145 degrees F due to the activity of thermophilic (heat-loving) and aerobic (air-loving) bacteria. They required careful attention to the proper balance between woody (carbonaceous) and high-nitrogen materials (manures and leafy greens) — a 30-40:1 ratio to be exact — as well as the amount of moisture and air throughout the pile. More importantly, thermophilic compost piles require frequent turning — once

a week or more — to "feed" the bacteria their dose of oxygen. None of this stopped me. Like many organic gardeners of that era, I made prodigious amounts of compost. Of course, I was underemployed and had plenty of time on my hands.

My near-religious fervor about composting has mellowed into a more even-handed approach toward this important part of the garden's cycle of decay and renewal. Today, instead of composting every kitchen scrap and every pruning, I separate them into different categories and treat each with the technology or technique that requires the least amount of effort.

Active composting a la 1970s is fast becoming a gardening relic. And here's the ultimate heresy: Some yard wastes need not be composted at all. There are more convenient ways to avoid throwing them away and still improve your yard. The idea is to choose the mix of options that's best for your lifestyle and budget.

Mulching Mowers

For many gardeners, raking, bagging and composting the never-ending stream of

ROBERT KOURIK *is the author of* Designing and Maintaining Your Edible Landscape Naturally.

lawn clippings is an occasion for some choice curses. But why bother? A "new" product, the mulching mower, allows you to skip the hassle not only of composting but also raking and bagging lawn clippings. The mulching mower was actually introduced some 30 years ago, but consumers weren't ready for it. A mulching mower has a specially designed blade and blade housing which finely chop the lawn clippings. In a mulching mower, the discharge chute which spews out the clippings is blocked off and they're blown back down into the turf where they decompose and help fertilize the lawn. Recent studies have shown that regular mowing when the grass is one to one-and-a-half inches taller than the cutting height may provide all the fertility your lawn requires. Not only that, but mulching mowers also save time — according to one study, seven hours over a six month period compared to regular mowing and bagging.

Some mulching mowers, called convertible mowers, enable you to capture clippings and leaves for composting when you want them. With convertible mowers you can have it either way, bagging clippings for composting or fertilizing your lawn.

All leading manufacturers of lawn mowers now offer one or more versions of a mulching mower. Some sell conversion kits for existing lawn mowers. The most important criterion for selecting a mulching mower is the engine's horsepower rating. These mowers need at least a four- or five-horsepower engine to move the blade quickly enough to achieve cutting, shredding *and* mulching.

Go to a local dealer. Take different models for a test mow. Be on the lookout for clogging, bunches of clippings on top of the grass and a ragged cut. The best cut is usually made by mowers with a doughnut-shaped blade housing. Other things to consider: How convenient is it to change the blade? How easy is it to attach and release the collection bag? Is the bag hung behind the mower instead of to the side, so it's easy to mow the edges of the lawn?

For a mulching mower, you'll spend from $200 to $500; convertible mulching mowers cost $250 to over $600.

Leaf Shredders

In the fall, deciduous trees produce a flurry of compostable material throughout much of the country. Leaves make a decent mulch or wonderful rich leaf mold when fully decomposed. But the blizzard of leaves in fall can overwhelm the most dedicated gardener.

One option is to use a dedicated leaf shredder to make the volume of leaves more manageable for mulching or composting. They're designed specifically to shred leaves and non-woody vegetable waste — not woody material, which should be shredded by a chipper.

There are several basic types of leaf shredders: leaf blowers which can be reversed to suck and shred the leaves and gasoline or electrically powered leaf shredders with either a filament or metal blade — called dedicated leaf shredders. Most manufacturers claim their leaf shredders can reduce ten bags of leaves to one bag of finely chopped material, for a 10:1 ratio. But studies indicate the true ratio of reduction is between 8:1 and 4:1 — still helpful.

Gas-powered shredders often require frequent cleaning of the air filter. On the other hand, electric shredders need an extension cord which can be a cumbersome bother in the landscape. Electric shredders tend to be slower than gasoline-powered models, although some slice and dice leaves as fast as the gas versions. Shredding thirty gallons of leaves can range from as fast as thirty to forty seconds to as long as four minutes. Always ask for a demonstration of the model you're considering to test the amount of reduction and speed. At the same time, note how much shredded material blows back out of the hopper and how much noise the shredder makes. Get

Combination chipper-shredders can turn a variety of garden wastes into valuable mulch.

Chippers are designed for woody wastes, which take forever to break down in a compost heap.

names from your local dealer of people who have purchased the model you're thinking about buying. And be sure to find out how well it works with wet leaves.

Other features to consider: Is the machine designed to protect your eyes and hands? Is a safe and useful tamper for pushing leaves into the mouth of the hopper included? Do you get protective goggles? How big is the mouth of the hopper? For a leaf shredder, expect to spend from $100 to $275.

You can avoid the expense of a shredder by heaping leaves in a huge wire-mesh cylinder in some hidden corner of your yard for one or two years. In some cities, leaves are picked up for free and composted; you can buy back the finished compost and avoid all the hassle of making your own. Plus, the leaves stay out of the landfill.

Chippers

Woody trimmings, which take forever to break down in a compost heap, can be chipped to cover a path or to use as a mulch. Most machines both chip and shred. The chipping is usually done in a side chute where branches and limbs are inserted into a rotating disk with fixed blades which shear off chips like carrots in a food processor. Shredding is done by carefully inserting the yard waste into a hopper on top of the machine where swinging or fixed hammers shred the material. The hammer-type machines usually have a sturdy screen covering the discharge port and all the material must be shredded to the same size as the screen before exiting. Because of the screen, this type of shredder is more likely to clog and stall than a knife-blade chipper. However, unlike knife-blade chippers, you can change the size of the discharge screen and therefore the size of the chips.

Buying a good quality chipper is no small investment — expect to pay at least $500, and up to $1300. A cheaper alternative is a very slow compost pile, more like a

Wooden compost bins are neat
but unnecessary.

The easiest way to compost is with a
free-standing pile.

crude heap, which will rot the woody waste if left alone long enough. Another consideration is whether you generate enough prunings to justify buying a chipper versus occasionally renting one. Remember, chippers are no fun to use — they rattle and shake, make a racket and are about the most dangerous garden tool.

The three most important considerations when buying a shredder or chipper are the engine's power, the sturdiness of the housing and the quality of the wheels.

Chippers come with either electric or gasoline engines. The latter are up to six times faster than the best electrical versions. However, electric models are quieter and vibrate less. If you opt for a gasoline-powered shredder, select a name-brand engine with the highest horsepower you can afford.

Make sure the housing is built with heavy-gauge metal, looks and feels sturdy and is well constructed. For example, avoid self-tapping screws in favor of nuts and bolts with lock washers. If the model has one, make sure the discharge screen covering the chipping mechanism is easy to change. Be sure it is easy to change the oil on the gas-powered models.

When testing a chipper at your local

A large cylinder or square made from
wire or snow fencing is an easy way to
keep your compost pile under control.

dealer, check to see if any material is thrown back out of the hopper, how well protected your hands are from the cutting mechanisms, how easy it is to get the last of the branches through the hoppers and how safe it is to use the tamper to push material through.

Other considerations: Will the machine chip the size and type of branches found in your yard? The typical chipper ad proclaims "Takes branches up to three inches thick!" But these ads seldom use the word "hardwood." And some studies found that the chipper could only handle the largest diameter mentioned in its literature if the branches were straight. Take samples of the wood you'll be chipping to the dealer and do a test run. Before buying, be sure to quiz others about their experiences. If possible, rent the machine you're thinking of buying and put it through its paces.

Chipper/shredders sell for $300 to as much as $1300. Many quality models in the $500 to $600 price range are available.

Composting Made Easy

After you've considered the above gizmos to determine the least time-consuming ways to manage your yard waste, it's time to consider the easiest way to compost what's left. Again, choose the least complicated options for your yard and lifestyle.

Binless Composting

With all the composting boxes, bins and cages on the market you'd think the Eleventh Commandment was "Thou shalt not compost without a store-bought gadget." Yet the easiest way to compost is with a freestanding pile. Just about any pile of organic matter will eventually rot if left to its own devices. But if you're just tossing stuff in a big "passive" compost heap, you'll need a large area for the heap's wide bottom. And, as with any kind of passive composting, what you get is not as rich as carefully layered and painstakingly turned hot compost, though it certainly will improve your soil's texture.

Bins from Pallets

Resourceful gardeners discovered long ago that wooden shipping pallets make cheap and effective compost bins. The gaps between the wooden slats help aerate the compost. Pallets are reused many times for shipping. When they're too battered to be useful any longer, they're often available for free — but always ask the shopkeeper first. Many gardeners simply lash each pallet to the next and leave the last one loosely attached to act as a door. Other gardeners install vertical posts in all four corners of the bin to support the pallets. A pallet can also be used on the bottom of a bin to help circulate air up through the bottom of the pile.

Compost Cylinders

Large cylinders made from ranch or snow fencing are easy ways to contain large passive compost piles. In fact, any type of flexible fencing, preferably with mesh or spaces to help aerate the pile, will do. Keep the height four feet or less to make it easy to toss the raw materials inside the cylinder. Put a wooden or metal fence post every two to three feet around the perimeter to support the wire. Leave one end of the fencing loosely tied to a post so this flap can be opened to remove the finished compost.

Cylinders, free-standing piles and pallet bins should be covered with a tarp to prevent the pile from getting soaked when it rains.

Designer Composters

If your taste leans toward a more expensive or ready-made composter, you have plenty of choices. Each one, of course, is advertised as the best solution to everybody's composting needs. The following discussion will help you sort out the hype.

The minimum volume for active composting is about one cubic yard (cy) (27 cubic feet (cf) or slightly more than 22 bushels) — depending on various factors. For example, active composting at the end of November in Michigan may necessitate three, four or five cubic yards of material to insulate enough of the pile from the cold weather to promote thermophilic activity. Passive compost piles, which don't have to heat up, can be smaller.

Many of the models listed below have no provision for protection from rain. You'll need to use a tarp, a wooden or metal lid or plastic sheeting to cover the composter for the best results.

Simple wire containers. Tidier than a free-form heap, quicker than building your own bin and able to contain a fair amount of compost, simple wire bins are perfect for the beginning composter. They're portable, economical, widely available from mail order companies and easy to assemble. You'll find many shapes for sale — square, hexagonal, round and pentagonal. The sizes range from from 15.5 to 23.7 cf.

All wire bins use galvanized metal mesh made from seven- to 14-gauge wire, and some have the added protection of a PVC coating. But some wire bins bend or bow out too easily. Each product is made from a different type of wire mesh; some are fairly sturdy, others are rather flimsy. The smaller the gauge number on the wire, the greater its strength. Consider how easy it is to open up the bin, to unload finished compost and to put the bin back together.

Individual wire bins cost from $30 to $50. Some models have extra panels for $19 to $32 which allow you to expand the capacity.

Wooden bin kits. Wooden compost bins come in two basic styles: with sides made of solid boards or of long, thin slats which are stacked horizontally like a log cabin. For an active compost pile, purchase only a model which allows you to take all the boards out from one side, starting from the top down.

Wooden bins have some serious limitations. First, they are vulnerable to gradual decay because the composting bacteria also eat away the wooden bin itself. Models made from rot-resistant woods like red-

wood or cedar are the only ones that will last. You can further slow decay by painting the wood with linseed oil or one of the new low-toxicity preservatives on the market, such as the one made by AFM. Don't use toxic wood preservatives which contain arsenic, creosote or pentachlorophenol, which can leach into your compost and contaminate your garden.

Second, wood warps and twists easily, especially the log-cabin style bin with long narrow slats. Once these warp, it is very difficult to re-insert the metal rods in the corners.

Most wooden bin kits hold from 20 to 29 cf. Prices for a wooden-slat model range from a low of about $79 to nearly $125. Solid-sided bins cost between $100 and $200.

Plastic compost bins. Plastic would seem to be the ultimate faux pas in an environmental garden. But compost bins made from plastic have some important advantages over wooden ones. Plastic bins don't rot, last a long time, don't warp from moisture and are lightweight and easy to move. Some are made from 50 to 100 percent postconsumer recycled plastic. Just make sure the plastic has an ultraviolet inhibitor to protect it from sunlight.

Most models have a sliding panel near the bottom for harvesting finished compost. Check this access panel to be sure there's enough slack for easy opening and closing. Several plastic composters come with three separate sections which can be re-stacked in reverse order when turning the pile.

Some mail order catalogs tout their plastic composters with "insulating walls." These are either one-quarter inch plastic walls, double walls or corrugated walls. The advertising copy claims such panels "promote heat retention for faster composting — even in cold weather" while, a little further down, maintaining that "the ventilation system ensures rapid decomposition." Get real guys! You can't have *both* excellent heat retention *and* air circulation, especially in cold weather.

Plastic bins don't rot or warp.
Some are even made of recycled
material.

The top of this kitchen waste digester
flips up so you can add food scraps
for earthworms and bacteria to digest.

Rotating composters are supposed to
make turning easier.
Some do, some don't.

One new plastic bin on the market is made of a plastic mesh cylinder with solid plastic interchangeable tops and bottoms, called dishes. Because the lips of the dishes fit snugly around the cylinder and the mesh has holes only three-eighths of an inch square, these bins are rat resistant. They're also very easy to use. The parts can be leapfrogged when turning the pile. To turn the pile inside the mesh cylinder you simply take the top dish off, set it nearby with the lip up, undo the carriage bolts on the front of the mesh cylinder, reassemble the mesh cylinder on what used to be the top dish, fill the cylinder with the partially composted material and cover with the remaining dish — which used to be the bottom dish. These models are made from 100 percent recycled plastic, come in 12 or 21 cf versions and cost from $50 to $130.

Tumbling composters. Rotating composters spin around their long axis and compost tumblers rotate top-to-bottom from

Red worms, which can be cultured in a small box indoors or outside,
turn kitchen scraps into a rich natural ferilizer.
The author's advice: Learn to love—or at least like—worms.

the midpoint of their long axis. Rotating or tumbling composters have the benefits, according to the catalogs, of "compost in just 21 days without the back strain of hand turning." But wet or moist compost is *much* heavier than it looks. To compensate for this weight, rotating bins often have a limited capacity (from seven to 11 cf). Still, some people have difficulty rotating the drum. Tumbling composters usually require squatting to either turn or harvest the compost. Some large rotating models hold up to 22 cf and have a geared drive to make the turning easier, but some people still have trouble cranking them.

Some rotating drums have lots of holes for aeration. Such composters tend to dry out the compost too quickly. And they require more attention to the proper carbon-to-nitrogen ratio.

Make sure the model you're thinking about buying is convenient to fill and empty. Some drums don't empty directly into a wheelbarrow or garden cart. Others are high enough to dump into a wheelbarrow, but the hatch is too high off the ground for easy loading.

Tumbling or rotating compost drums cost from $100 to nearly $400.

What to Do With Kitchen Wastes

Kitchen scraps make a rich compost, but they're about the most awkward compostables to deal with. They can attract insects and rodents. If improperly disposed of, they can also smell. Most kitchen scraps can be added to hot compost piles. If you've got a passive compost heap — or no compost pile at all — the simplest way to deal with kitchen wastes is to bury them in trenches or holes throughout the garden with a cover of at least eight inches of soil. But this doesn't help much in small yards or where winter temperatures freeze the ground solid.

Kitchen Waste Digesters

These are among the newer inventions. They're usually cone-shaped with dark green or black sides to help heat up the scraps to promote dehydration, which decreases the bulk, and bacterial digestion. Some have a plastic basket which is buried in the ground just below the cone to help fend off racoons, mice and rats.

Kitchen waste digesters have a few limitations: If conditions are right, bacteria and earthworms digest the wastes; if not, you get a small, slimy pile of wastes which have been decomposed anaerobically. In either case, you bury what's left when the digester is full and must be moved. The digesters are not usually free of fruit flies as the manufacturers claim. Rats sometimes chew through the plastic basket to eat the waste. The digesters shouldn't be used where a high water table would flood the soil beneath the cone. In a large household, the device can fill up within four or five months. And when you move the cone to bury the rotted material, the smell can be intense if the wastes have gone anaerobic.

Worm Bins

Red worms (*Lumbricus rubellus*) have practically insatiable appetites for kitchen scraps and produce nutrient-rich worm castings. And worms can be cultured in fairly small boxes inside the house, in the basement, root cellar, garage or even the kitchen year-round.

Over the years, worms have become my preferred method of converting kitchen scraps into valuable fertilizer. I know, I know — some people need years of therapy to get beyond their aversion to slimy, snake-like things. My advice is to learn to love, or at least like, worms! They're one of nature's grand cultivators and decomposers. They're quite tame creatures with fascinating habits. Best of all, they produce a concentrated, highly desirable fertilizer — not just a soil amendment like a passive compost pile or the various compost-in-a-black-plastic-bag techniques recommended for city gardeners.

To start, you need a two-pound coffee can's worth of worms. (Most gardening magazines have classified sections with listings of mail order worms.) Worm bins should be kept in a cool area where temperatures stay between 55 and 75 degrees F. Properly managed worm bins are odor free. ⊕

THE FLIP SIDE OF COMPOST

What's in It, Where to Use It and Why

by Richard M. Kashmanian

and Joseph M. Keyser

Gardeners like to think of themselves as nurturing types — hands in the soil, coaxing riches from the earth. We tend to forget that our gardens are linked ever so closely to the local landfill. Every time we rake leaves or lawn clippings, deadhead or prune, bag it up and leave it on the curb, we're contributing to that enormous environmental problem known as "municipal solid waste." In fact, according to the U.S. Environmental Protection Agency (EPA), yard trimmings account for almost one-fifth of what ends up in landfills — about 31 million tons a year. Combined with kitchen food scraps, they represent about 28 percent.

Richard M. Kashmanian, PhD, *is a Senior Economist in the Office of Policy, Planning and Evaluation of the U.S. Environmental Protection Agency.*
Joseph M. Keyser *is Director of Programs of the American Horticultural Society, and the designer of its National Home Composting Park in Alexandria, Virginia.*

Fortunately, there's an easy way not only to keep this stuff out of overburdened landfills but at the same time make our gardens healthier, lusher and more productive — by using compost. Off-the-shelf composters, leaf shredders, mulching mowers and a host of other new garden equipment is making it ever easier to recycle yard trimmings and kitchen scraps in our own backyards. But beyond that, by buying compost at the garden center and using it as a soil amendment, mulch and natural source of nutrients, gardeners can help boost the fledgling compost industry and thus encourage environmentally sound uses of other organic residues as well, from livestock manures to fish byproducts to municipal sewage sludge.

The Garbage Problem

Americans throw away about 180 million tons of municipal solid waste each year. EPA estimates that in 1988, 73 percent of this ended up in landfills, 14 percent was incinerated and 13 percent was recycled. Only one percent was made into compost. If soiled paper were added to the yard trimmings and kitchen scraps, up to 30 to 60 percent of all discards could potentially be composted in specially designed facilities; this paper probably wouldn't be recycled back into paper products.

Why does so much compostable material get shipped off to landfills and incinerators, with their environmental problems, when it can be used to enrich our gardens? That's a question increasingly asked by the government officials who must deal with the garbage glut. Some states have taken ambitious steps to encourage composting. Fifteen have already established bans on some or all kinds of yard trimmings from landfills. Eight of these bans were in effect as of January 1, 1992: Connecticut (leaves), Florida (leaves, grass, woody materials), Illinois (leaves, grass, prunings), Iowa (leaves, grass, wood chips), Minnesota (leaves, grass, prunings), Missouri (leaves, grass, Christmas trees), New Jersey (leaves) and Pennsylvania (leaves, prunings). The bans in the seven other states — Arkansas, Massachusetts, Michigan, North Carolina, Ohio, South Carolina and Wisconsin — will go into effect by mid-1995. More than 40 percent of the American population lives in these states. In many states, local governments are collecting the yard trimmings from homeowners and setting up large-scale facilities where they are turned into compost. In other states, private companies are also building and running composting operations.

If nobody uses all this compost, these efforts will collapse. And that's how gardeners can help. "Residential users" — that is, gardeners — are one of the largest markets for compost in the country.

The Benefits of Compost

Compost, a relatively stable humus product, is an excellent soil conditioner or amendment. It's rich in organic matter. It also contains a modest amount of the "big three"

RICHARD KASHMANIAN

To ease the pressure on overburdened landfills, local governments and private companies are getting into the composting business. Above and at right are typical composting facilities. By using compost, gardeners can encourage environmentally sound uses of discarded leaves, lawn clippings and other organic "wastes."

nutrients — nitrogen, phosphorus and potassium — although the exact nutrient level depends on the materials composted and how they are composted (see Table 1). Compost provides additional macronutrients, such as calcium, magnesium and sulfur, and micronutrients like copper, iron, manganese and zinc, which generally are not available in chemical fertilizers. It is typically dark brown to black in color, crumbly

Before: the raw materials.

Plastic bags and other debris are removed.

After: brown gold for the garden.

and earthy smelling. You can make it in your own backyard, pick it up for free at some municipal composting facilities or buy it from private and agricultural composting operations, in addition to garden centers and other retail outlets.

Using compost improves the soil's biological, chemical and physical properties, ultimately improving the soil's fertility. It's especially beneficial when incorporated in clay and sandy soils. Adding compost to clay soils reduces soil density and compaction

TABLE 1

APPROXIMATE NUTRIENT AND pH VALUES FOR DIFFERENT TYPES OF COMPOST

COMPOST TYPE	NITROGEN (% DRY WT)	PHOSPHORUS (% DRY WT)	POTASSIUM (% DRY WT)	TOTAL pH
Yard trimmings	0.1 %- 2.0 %	0.03%- 1.0 %	0.04%- 3.8 %	5.7- 7.6
Livestock manure	0.5 %- 3.0 %	0.1 %- 4.0 %	0.5 %- 3.0 %	8.0- 9.0
Municipal sewage sludge	1.0 %- 1.5 %	0.4 %- 2.0 %	0.2 %- 0.4 %	7.2- 8.0
Fish byproducts	0.6%- 5.1%	0.1%-2.0%	0.6%	8.0

and improves soil porosity, aeration and drainage. Water and plant roots can penetrate more deeply. The upper soil layer is less saturated, so there's less danger of root rot.

Adding compost to sandy soils binds together soil particles, improving their ability to retain moisture and nutrients, withstand drought and resist erosion. Plant growth is improved because more water is available for root uptake and soluble nutrients don't leach quickly through the soil. Leaching nutrients can pollute the groundwater. Less leaching also means you won't have to use as much fertilizer, or as often.

Adding compost also increases the soil's cation exchange capacity (CEC), and thus its natural fertility. When the soil's CEC is improved, it is better able to attract and hold positively charged nutrients, including calcium, magnesium, nitrogen and potassium. These plant nutrients are therefore less likely to leach into the groundwater.

Compost typically has a pH of 7.0 to 8.0 (see Table 1). Slightly alkaline compost reduces the need to add lime in some gar-den situations. However, if you're using it on soils where acid-loving plants are grown (that is, plants which prefer a soil pH of less than 6), be sure to apply it with an acid-rich mulch like coffee grounds, pine bark, sawdust, shredded oak leaves or wood ash.

Compost has other advantages. Organic materials and nutrients are returned to the soil. Soil tilth and structure are improved. There is less crusting, making it easier for seedlings to emerge. The soil is easier to work, and soil temperatures are moderated. Increasing the soil's organic content creates a favorable environment for earthworms and increases the soil microbial activity that fosters plant growth. Some composts can even suppress plant diseases. This in turn reduces the need for chemical pesticides and the potential pollution that results when water washes them into waterways or groundwater supplies. And properly processed compost is largely free of pathogens and weed seeds.

Last, but still very important, is the fact that compost releases nitrogen slowly

T A B L E   2
HOW MUCH COMPOST TO APPLY

Plant/Soil Application	Compost Application Rate
New lawns	1"-2" mixed into top 4"-6" of soil
Reseeded lawns	1" mixed into top 2"-3" of soil
Topdressing for existing lawns	1/8"-1/4" spread uniformly
Topdressing for vegetables, flowers, shrubs	1"-2" spread uniformly; if spread 3"-4" deep, check for sowbugs
Ground cover and annual planting beds	3" mixed into top 6" of soil
Garden soil	1"-3" mixed into top 6"-8" of soil
Incorporation around shrubs	3" mixed into top 6" of soil
Potting mix	25%-30% by volume
Mulch for deciduous trees, rose beds	3"-4" spread uniformly
Mulch for vegetables, annual and perennial planting beds	2"-3" spread uniformly
Mulch for exposed slopes	2"-4" of coarse compost (3/4"-1 1/2") spread uniformly

NOTE: The application rates in this table represent ranges reported in the published literature on compost. Approximately 1,000 pounds of compost is equivalent to one cubic yard of compost. One inch of compost spread over one acre is equivalent to approximately 65 tons of compost at a 40% moisture content. Where appropriate, these rates represent annual applications.

because almost all of the nutrients are in organic forms. The organic nitrogen must be converted to inorganic ammonium and oxidized to nitrate to become available to plants. On average, approximately 10 percent (and as high as 20 percent) of the nitrogen is released during the first year, 5 percent the second year and 2 percent each year thereafter. (About 25 to 40 percent of the phosphorus and 70 percent of the potassium are available during the first year.) These estimates vary according to soil aeration, moisture and temperature. This slow release of nitrogen is often better synchronized with the nutrient needs of the growing plant.

Quick-release chemical fertilizers are more apt than composts to create an oversupply of nitrogen in the soil which can lead to leaching of nitrates and groundwater pollution. The excess nitrates can also pollute water runoff and end up in rivers, lakes and streams. However, even when you use compost you should grow winter cover plants (alfalfa, clovers, rye, vetch) to absorb nitrates that may otherwise wash away once the growing season is over.

Composted organic materials are usually preferable to uncomposted organic materials as a source of organic matter. The compost is relatively stable humus, whereas soil organisms must decompose the uncomposted organic material before its nutrients are released. If you add uncomposted material rich in carbon (such as leaves and sawdust) to your soil, you may need to add nitrogen because as the soil microbes decompose it they tie up nitrogen that would otherwise be available to the growing plants. Uncomposted (or not fully composted) materials are best incorporated during the fall to allow enough time for the soil to season them before spring planting.

Using Compost in the Garden

You can use compost in a variety of ways — as a soil conditioner or amendment throughout the garden, as a lawn topdressing, in potting soils, as a germination or rooting medium and as a mulch. It can replace peat moss, which has to be taken from somewhere else and therefore impoverishes another ecosystem to improve your garden. Compost also can replace or reduce the need for potting mixes, chemical fertilizers, lime and other soil amendments, chemical pesticides and inorganic mulches.

A compost's particle size helps determine its use. For example, a fine compost (less than seven-sixteenths of an inch) should be used as a topdressing (if incorporated into the top one to two inches of topsoil it is unlikely to wash away in a rainstorm), in

a potting mix or as a soil amendment. A coarse compost (seven-sixteenths of an inch or greater) is best used as a mulch.

Seasoned compost can comprise up to 25 to 30 percent by volume of a potting mix. Higher levels can cause waterlogging and poor aeration and necessitate amendments like perlite to improve drainage.

When used as a topdressing for lawns, compost increases the earthworm population and encourages deep root growth.

Mulch helps the soil retain moisture by reducing evaporation. It minimizes soil spattering from rainfall and therefore the spread of soil-borne diseases. It reduces compaction and soil erosion (even on steep slopes), suppresses weeds (especially if applied after weeding) and moderates soil temperature. Mulch improves the environment for earthworms and thus helps aerate the soil. It also returns organic matter to the soil as it breaks down.

How Much Compost?

How much compost you should apply (see Table 2) depends on the fertility of your soil, the specific use of the compost, the type of compost, the needs of your plants and the time of year. If the compost is bagged, follow the directions on the label. Give the soil about a month to fully condition the compost before you plant.

When applied as a mulch, compost should be spread within one to two inches from the base of the plant to beyond the plant's drip line. Heavily mulch plants with shallow roots (for example, rhododendrons and azaleas) for the winter months to protect them from freezing and soil upheaval. Some of the mulch should be removed in early spring so the soil can warm up and encourage early season root growth and development. ⊕

The views expressed in this article are the opinions of the authors, not the official policy of the U.S. Environmental Protection Agency.

XERISCAPING DEMYSTIFIED

This water-conserving California garden includes a lush assortment of native plants and non-natives from similar climates around the world.

A WATER MISER'S GUIDE TO GARDENING

BY BOB HYLAND

Xeriscaping is the unfortunate term for gardening that uses water sparingly. In fact, more than one wit has called it "zeroscaping" — conjuring up images of gardens with nothing but gravel and cacti. Yet xeriscapes need not

BOB HYLAND *is Director of Education for Strybing Arboretum and Botanical Gardens in Golden Gate Park, San Francisco. He also sells water-wise perennials and shrubs at Magic Gardens Nursery in Berkeley.*

be dull, dusty landscapes consisting of sparse plantings in a sea of pebbles. No matter where you live, you can have a water-thrifty garden with a lush diversity of native and exotic plants from similar climates across the country and around the world.

Like the term xeriscaping, the principles of low-water landscaping evolved in the Desert Southwest. Drought, heat and water restrictions have taught gardeners in Arizona, New Mexico and other arid states to grow drought-tolerant plants, install low-volume irrigation systems and design gardens zoned according to water needs.

Here in Northern California, specifically the San Francisco Bay Area, gardeners have endured five years of winter drought. In San Francisco's Mediterranean climate we can normally expect 22 to 24 inches of rainfall between November 1 and April 30, followed by six months of dryness. Most plants have to be irrigated during the summer dry period. The current drought has severely depleted reservoirs and groundwater supplies and ended our ability to water gardens and lawns indiscriminately — forever! Yet xeriscaping is still not that well understood or widely practiced.

Gardeners in regions with more abundant water supplies and more reliable, evenly spaced rainfall have been even slower to embrace xeriscaping. But periodic spells of summer drought, short-term water restrictions and difficult-to-forecast climate changes have hit almost every section of the country in recent years. Xeriscaping makes good environmental sense for gardeners everywhere.

Xeriscaping has six, easy-to-understand concepts:
◆ Use common-sense design by grouping plants with similar water requirements.
◆ Limit turf areas.
◆ Grow water-efficient plants suited to your climate.
◆ Irrigate efficiently and conservatively.
◆ Improve the water-holding capacity of your soils.
◆ Use water-conserving mulches.

Common-Sense Design

At Strybing Arboretum and Botanical Gardens in Golden Gate Park, San Francisco, we demonstrate many xeriscaping techniques to the public. We group plants according to their geographic origins and water requirements. Plants from the various Mediterranean climates — around the Mediterranean Sea, Cape Province of South Africa, southwestern Australia and California — are grown together in landscaped collections. Generally, plants from these regions have adapted to summer drought conditions.

You can adapt this principle for your home garden. Group plants not only by similar needs of sun, shade, soil type and pH (acidity or alkalinity) but by water needs as well. Look carefully at your garden and you'll discover it has several microclimates caused by different conditions of sun and shade, ground slope, available moisture and air movement. Map these areas and use them to divide your yard into low, moderate and high water-use zones. Any lawn area will be a zone of high water use, which is why limiting the amount of turf grass is so important. Even here at the Botanical Gardens, turf areas are used sparingly and limited in size; large, mulched planting beds predominate.

Select plants for the moderate water-use zone based on how much irrigation they will require when they're mature. Irrigation is needed weekly during the establishment of new plantings from containers, but once settled in (generally after one year), the plants in this zone should require less frequent watering. Locate the moderate water zone close to the house to take advantage of runoff from downspouts, driveways, patios and decks, and of graywater collected from the shower or laundry to provide additional water.

The low water-use zone is reserved for plants which, once established, require little if any water other than that provided by normal rainfall (and in coastal California by fog). In San Francisco's Botanical Gardens many slopes and boundary areas are planted with evergreen, shrubby, native California chaparral species like manzanitas (*Arctostaphylos* spp.), California lilacs (*Ceanothus* spp.) and fremontia (*Fremontodendron californicum*), which require little or no summer irrigation.

Limit Turf Areas

The general recommendation for the average single family lot in California is 800 square feet or less of irrigated lawn. Of course, yards in San Francisco (and cities across the country) are much smaller and require considerably less lawn. Inner city gardeners should seriously consider doing without grass — it's thirsty stuff and requires weekly mowing and other maintenance to keep it attractive.

Design your lawn as an oasis of green on fairly level ground to prevent water runoff and locate it close to decks or patios for high visual impact. Here in Northern California we recommend coarse, deep-rooted, tall fescue grass mixes that are better able to pull moisture from the soil and stay green with less frequent irrigation. In the Botanical Gardens, we also encourage the planting of ground covers as alternatives to turf grasses, such as woolly thyme (*Thymus pseudolanuginosus*), blue star creeper (*Laurentia fluviatilis*), stonecrops (*Sedum* spp.), prostrate myoporum (*Myoporum parvifolium*) and creeping rosemary (*Rosmarinus officinalis* 'Prostratus'). Many of these have soft textures like the turf grasses and can tolerate light foot traffic.

Grow Water-Efficient Plants

"Water-efficient," "drought tolerant," "water-wise" and "water-thrifty" are all apt descriptions of the type of plants you should consider for your garden. A wide range of beautiful plants including trees, shrubs, flowering perennials, ground covers and bunchgrasses fit the description — not just cacti and succulents!

Choose plants that are adapted to cope with reduced irrigation. Silver or gray foliage that reflects sunlight, cools the plant and reduces water loss is one such adaptation. Plants that develop deep root systems, especially a single taproot, are also capable of surviving with less watering.

In private California gardens we have visited on tours sponsored by Strybing Arboretum & Botanical Gardens, I've seen shrubs such as California lilac (*Ceanothus* 'Julia Phelps'), purple hop bush (*Dodonaea viscosa* 'Purpurea') and pineapple guava (*Feijoa sellowiana*) look remarkably attractive with little to no summer watering. In fact, some members of the *Ceanothus* genus are so sensitive to summer water that one or two irrigations will kill them outright.

Likewise, perennials such as *Penstemon* 'Midnite' and *P.* 'Huntington Pink', Russian sage (*Perovskia atriplicifolia*), dwarf lavenders (*Lavandula angustifolia* 'Hidcote'), hybrid lavender (*Lavandula* 'Quasti'), lamb's ear (*Stachys byzantina* 'Silver Carpet'), red-hot pokers (*Kniphofia uvaria*) and green lavender-cotton (*Santolina virens*) bloom their heads off and/or display showy foliage with infrequent irrigation.

Wherever you live and garden you should be able to find plant lists based on low-water requirements. The plants may be a bit different from those in the pages of most English and East Coast-biased gardening books, so you may need to open your eyes to a new aesthetic. Check with local water agencies, horticultural libraries at public gardens, Cooperative Extension offices, state departments of water resources or state and national xeriscape councils for suggestions. Better yet, visit demonstration xeriscapes at botanical gardens, parks and water district offices.

Irrigate Efficiently

Here at the Botanical Gardens we teach four steps to efficient irrigation. We realize that it's difficult to change over to a low-volume watering system in an established landscape. When you're replacing areas of a garden, consider retrofitting the irrigation system to apply the correct amount of water.

◆ Separate irrigation lines into the high, moderate and low water-use zones that you've delineated in your garden plan and set an automatic valve at the head of each line. High use lines should be equipped with spray heads; moderate use lines should use bubbler and shrub spray heads. Low water-use lines should have drip emitters that supply water at a slow rate, reducing runoff and allowing for deep watering. Soaker hoses that are less expensive and easier to install are an alternative type of drip system. Drip irrigation applies water only where needed — at the base of the plant, which encourages good root growth.

◆ For turf grass (or lawn substitute) areas, overlap sprinkler spray patterns so that water from one head reaches out to the next nearest head. Ask your irrigation supplier for sprinkler heads that have "matched precipitation rates" and which put out "low gallonage."

◆ Tie each valve into an automatic timer to control how many minutes each applies water. Select a timer that allows recycling — several cycles of on/off "run time" during each irrigation day.

◆ Prepare and follow an irrigation schedule. Water your garden during the cool times of the day to reduce evaporation. Ask your local water utility for tips.

Improve Your Soil

Here in the San Francisco Bay Area we have a variety of soil types with varying water needs. Parts of the city have clay soils that absorb water slowly and cause surface runoff; other neighborhoods nearer the ocean and bay have sandy soils that dry rapidly and leach nutrients away quickly from plant roots.

My advice to gardeners is to learn about the composition of your soils. You can purchase a soil test kit and do your own analysis or you can usually send soil samples to testing laboratories or your county Cooperative Extension office. These tests will answer questions about soil structure, pH, micronutrients and general fertility.

There are many organic amendments that can be applied to improve your soil. Home composting is one of the most ecological ways for gardeners to have a ready source of organic matter for soil improvement. At the Botanical Gardens soil amendments such as fir and redwood mulches,

Scaevola 'Mauve Clusters', left, is a handsome, drought-tolerant substitute for thirsty lawn in a California garden. Below, drip irrigation emitters apply water where it's needed—on new plantings.

BOB HYLAND

BOB HYLAND

To save water, limit the size of your lawn
and use large mulched planting beds instead.

peat, wood shavings and compost are all used in different plant collections, depending on the needs of those plants. Our redwood grove is a self-sustaining ecosystem that continually freshens its own soil through the buildup and decomposition of needles shed by the mighty coastal redwoods (*Sequoia sempervirens*).

At the Botanical Gardens most of our grass clippings, weeds, chipped tree prunings and other organic waste is hauled to a central composting site located in Golden Gate Park. Finished compost is then readily available to our gardeners when needed. Another San Francisco gardening organization that offers composting demonstrations and a wealth of literature is San Francisco League of Urban Gardeners (S.L.U.G.). Many cities have similar community-based gardening groups who can provide advice on composting.

Use Mulches

Mulched planting beds are an ideal replace-ment for water-guzzling lawns. Mulches cover and cool the soil and minimize evaporation of soil moisture. When applied to a depth of two to three inches, mulches eliminate weed growth and help slow erosion. As they decompose and are turned into the soil, they improve soil tilth and fertility.

There are many organic mulches to choose from. Compost makes a great mulch. The most commonly used mulches are bark chips in a variety of sizes and shredded tree mulches, typically redwood and fir here in Northern California. Other mulches include cocoa hulls and wood shavings.

The bottom line is that xeriscaping uses water wisely and conservatively in any type of climate, be it here in California or New York. We all need to conscientiously practice its water-saving principles. Whether you're starting a garden from scratch at the drawing board or gradually retrofitting an established "water-dependent" landscape, I encourage you to think "less water" before you plant. ⊕

An Environmental Gardener's Guide to

PEST MANAGEMENT

by Craig Hollingsworth

and Karen Idoine

Since the first seeds were gathered and deliberately planted, pests have been the bane of gardeners. Over time, we have created many of our own pest problems. By concentrating crops at one site, we've made food more accessible for pests. As a result, they reproduce more quickly. Whenever we till the soil, we create a hospitable environment for weed seeds to germinate and grow. We've imported pests from around the globe — without the natural enemies that keep them in check. More commonly, we've made pest problems worse by using pesticides indiscriminately. In fact, on a per acre basis, more pesticide is applied to home gardens than to farms in the United States.

Craig Hollingsworth *is an Extension Specialist with the Massachusetts Integrated Pest Management Program.*
Karen Idoine *is a Horticultural Agent with Massachusetts Cooperative Extension who also contributes a gardening column to the* Boston Globe.

We know that pesticides can cause environmental problems. What isn't so obvious is that they also cause horticultural problems. Killing the natural enemies of a pest may lead to later, more severe outbreaks of the same pest. Pesticides can also kill the natural enemies of other organisms, causing outbreaks of still more pests. Repeated pesticide use often makes the pests become resistant to the pesticides, so that ever higher doses are required. Problems — largely from pesticide use — have led to a new concept of managing pests called "integrated pest management" or IPM.

Ecological Pest Management

Integrated pest management is an ecologically based approach to pest control. Fields, gardens or lawns aren't automatically treated with weekly or routine sprays "just in case." Even the discovery of a pest doesn't automatically trigger a control action; instead, the plants are checked regularly to make sure the pests aren't present in numbers large enough to do significant damage. IPM is a decision-making process. Using an IPM approach you decide what causes the problem, if you need to do something, what you need to do and when to do it.

Properly practiced, IPM includes a combination of sensible pest controls and preventive measures that minimize adverse effects to the environment while protecting the plant. IPM is an opportunity to practice backyard ecology, to understand the interaction of all living organisms in a garden environment — not just the plants.

How to Start

To start your IPM program, you need a plan. What is your objective: to have a healthy, safe, bountiful garden? To produce perfect, undamaged plants for flower shows? To nurture a variety of plant and animal species for your enjoyment? To minimize your use of pesticides? To use no pesticides at all? Your objectives will help determine which mix of management techniques is best for you. Often, you'll have several conflicting objectives and you'll need to compromise. Once you've set your priorities, there are a few basic procedures to follow:

◆ Learn about the pests and problems associated with each crop or planting in your area. Don't wait until pests appear, as many problems can be avoided simply with proper plant selection and garden design. Different pests require different methods of control, depending on their life cycle, habits and physiology.

◆ Monitor your plants or crop at regular intervals to see how many pests are present and what kind of damage is being done.

◆ Establish a threshold for damage. In agricultural IPM programs, farmers use precisely defined "economic thresholds" to determine when to treat pest populations. These are based on the value of the crop, the damage caused and the cost of treatment. Gardeners can use a similar process for determining when and what treatment is required. Is the damage tolerable? Is it serious enough to warrant action? The action itself will depend on the degree of damage or potential damage. A few Japanese beetles may warrant hand-picking, while greater numbers might justify treating the beetle grubs in the lawn while they are small and vulnerable.

◆ Combine management strategies that complement each other. For instance, resistant plants, proper site selection, biological controls and physical barriers all reduce pest damage, but when combined, or integrated, provide even greater protection. Keep in mind that a garden is a refuge for many living organisms. Most of them aren't pests, but rather useful inhabitants which enhance the garden by decomposing dead plants, pollinating, preying on pests or providing food or shelter for other useful organisms. Select management practices least harmful to all of the organisms in your garden.

◆ Keep notes on what you see — the level of damage, the action you take, what works and what doesn't. They will prove immensely helpful in the future.

Choosing Strategies that Work

The tools of IPM include cultural practices, biological controls, physical controls, traps and chemical controls. The best courses of action will vary according to local conditions and your own objectives.

Cultural Practices

Cultural practices are growing techniques which make the garden less favorable to pests, thereby reducing the need for more expensive and disruptive controls. Practices will vary with the type of garden or planting. Some cultural controls are:

Don't just reach for the dust or spray. Handpicking, applications of *B.t.* and row covers are less toxic caterpillar controls.

This yellow pan trap will let you know when the first aphids of the season arrive.

Put predators to work in your garden. Here, a stinkbug nymph attacks a Colorado potato beetle.

◆ **PEST-RESISTANT SPECIES AND CULTI-VARS.** Look for plants without pest problems and cultivars bred specifically for pest resistance. For example, shade gardeners in the Northeast can reduce insect problems by planting witch-hazel, bayberry and other insect-resistant shrubs[1]. Apple growers can significantly reduce fungicide use by selecting disease-resistant cultivars.

◆ **LIGHT AND AIR CIRCULATION.** Choosing a site with good air circulation can reduce the need for fungicide on susceptible plants. Pruning and wide plant spacing promote air penetration and movement, further reducing disease problems. Trees

[1] See "Insect Resistant Shrubs" by R.J. Gouger in *Gardening in the Shade*, Brooklyn Botanic Garden Record, Handbook #61.

Keep weeds down—and conserve water—with mulch.

Proper site selection can be critical. Because the tree on the left is in shade part of the day, it is less susceptible to white pine weevil attack.

Row covers moderate temperature and keep out pests.

around gardens or lawns can be thinned or pruned to allow more light to penetrate. On the other hand, dense plantings keep the weed population down. Apparent conflicts of this type are common in IPM, but they can be resolved by weighing the potential benefits and consequences of both actions.

◆ **SANITATION.** Removing dead or infected plant parts from the garden reduces the spread of potential diseases and other pests.

◆ **CULTIVATION.** In most garden situations, herbicides are not necessary; weeds can be controlled simply by hand cultivation. The secret is timing — one well timed cultivation won't take any more time than spraying an herbicide but can save hours of struggle with overgrown weeds. Usually, the best time to cultivate is when weeds are small and succulent, before seeds have set. Spend some time choosing a comfortable, easy-to-use hand cultivater.

Biological Controls

When you introduce a pest's natural enemies into your garden or try to get them to come naturally by creating a hospitable environment, you're using a biological control. Natural enemies can be predators, parasites or diseases. You can increase populations of natural enemies by providing them with shelter and additional food sources — nectar-producing plants, dill, coriander, caraway and other plants in the parsley family, for example. Minimizing pesticide use also helps.

Some natural enemies, such as nematodes, ladybird beetles and Trichogramma parasitic wasps, are available for purchase. It's important to select the right natural enemy for the specific pest and to release it under the right conditions. For example, nematodes require moist organic soils. If you purchase ladybird beetles that have just come out of hibernation, they may require a flight period before settling down to feed; and when they do settle down, it may be in someone else's yard.

Some natural enemies are general feeders while others are more specific. Ladybird beetles feed on many soft-bodied insects, while Trichogramma wasps generally attack the eggs of moths and butterflies. Preying mantids are such general feeders that they will attack almost any insect — including pollinators and natural enemies.

The use of diseases to control insect pests is becoming increasingly effective. The bacterium *Bacillus thuringiensis*, or *B.t.*, is marketed under several trade names, including Dipel and Biobit. *B.t.* attacks specific insect groups, depending on the variety selected. *B.t.* products are available for control of caterpillars, Colorado potato beetle, elm leaf beetle, fungus gnats and biting flies. Be sure to purchase the right strain for the pest you're trying to control. Because *B.t.* is so specific in its action it is very safe for humans and does not interfere with other management practices.

Physical Controls and Traps

Physical controls include hand picking, mulches, barriers and even vacuum systems that suck up pests.

◆ MULCHES. In addition to conserving water, mulches are an excellent nontoxic weed control. In the home garden, plastic or fabric mulches eventually lead to disposal problems. Organic mulches which break down in the soil, contribute to the build-up of humus and provide shelter for predators (especially spiders) are probably a better choice. Because mulches may also provide a moist habitat for slugs, clean cultivation may be the best option where slugs are a problem.

◆ **ROW COVERS.** Another multi-purpose horticultural tool, spun-bonded polypropylene fabric row covers are used primarily as frost protection, growth enhancers and season extenders. Used during pest activity periods, they can also prevent pests from infesting small fruit and vegetable crops.

◆ **TRAPS.** You can use traps to monitor pests or to reduce pest populations. They work by using visual, odor and sexual cues to attract insect pests.

Visual traps mimic the light waves of a host plant, but the color is more intense than the real thing. Thus, a yellow trap, a mimic of green foliage, is more attractive to the insect than the foliage itself. A common visual trap in the Northeast is the red sphere. The sphere attracts apple maggot flies by mimicking a red apple. During the period when apple maggot flies are in flight, the trap is larger and redder than the apples and therefore more attractive. Home gardeners can eliminate sprays against apple maggot by placing five red spheres in each apple tree. Other visual traps include white and blue cards, which attract different pests in different situations (for example, tarnished plant bugs are attracted to white cards, greenhouse thrips to blue cards).

Another common trap in the Northeast is the Japanese beetle trap, which is baited with sexual and floral attractants to lure beetles away from flowers and other plantings. Because these traps attract more beetles into an area, make sure you place them far enough away and downwind from plantings to avoid making the beetle infestation even worse. Generally these traps are useless in neighborhoods with large resident beetle populations. In a country setting, where the beetle population is less widespread, traps placed well away from the crop to be protected may be of some value.

You can buy traps for slugs or make them yourself using shallow pans or jar lids

FOR MORE INFORMATION
· ·
IPM programs often depend on specific information. Some of this information can be obtained through your local Cooperative Extension office.

The following books are good references:
Common Sense Pest Control: Least Toxic Solutions for Your Home, Garden, Pets and Community by William Olkowski, Sheila Daar and Helga Olkowski. 1991, Box 5506, Taunton Press, Newtown, CT 06470-5506.

Pests of the Garden and Small Farm: A Grower's Guide to Using Less Pesticide by Mary Louise Flint. 1990, University of California Publications, 6701 San Pablo Ave., Oakland, CA 94608-1239.

sunk to ground level and baited with beer. A "roof" made from a cottage cheese container can reduce evaporation and keep rain from diluting the beer.

Chemical Controls
For some pests, there is no adequate cultural, physical or biological control; pesticides are the remaining option.

Pesticides should be selected and applied in a way that causes the least environmental disruption and the least impact on beneficial and other non-target species. Again, combining other management techniques with the use of a pesticide will be more effective than relying on the chemical alone.

Be careful when you use any kind of pesticide. Even "organic" or naturally occurring pesticides are toxic (see the article that follows). Insecticidal and herbicidal

Attract beneficial insects by adding fennel and other plants of the parsley family to your garden.

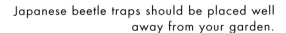

Japanese beetle traps should be placed well away from your garden.

soaps are relatively non-toxic to humans, but they can affect a wide range of species, including beneficial insects. Whenever possible, they should be applied directly to the pest, as a spot treatment. When using soaps, look for phytotoxic reactions. Tissues of some plants react adversely to soaps, causing spotting, browning, or even plant death.

A pesticide is more effective if the application is timed to treat the most sensitive stage of the pest. Knowledge of the pest and its life cycle is therefore important.

For example, non-toxic horticultural oils can smother mite eggs while more toxic pesticides are ineffective against eggs. These oils are highly refined, and under conditions of moderate temperature and low humidity, can be applied to most ornamental and some vegetable crops, even in summer.

Pesticides are usually formulated specifically for specific pests on specific plants. Before using a pesticide READ THE LABEL and make sure that it's the right pesticide for the situation. ⊕

NATURAL PESTICIDES

ARE THEY REALLY SAFER?

BY CHERYL BEST

Sod Webworm Moth

Public concern over the safety of pesticides has prompted more and more companies to develop natural pest controls, including natural chemical pesticides derived from plants. Because safety appears to be the chief reason behind the growing market for natural pesticides, it's logical to ask just how safe are they?

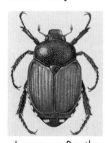

Japanese Beetle

To answer this question, it's necessary to define the word "safe." One aspect of safety concerns a pesticide's potential impact on the environment. Does it pollute groundwater supplies? Does it contaminate the soil? Will it injure or kill fish, birds, mammals or beneficial insects? How long does it persist in the environment? The other aspect of safety

concerns human health. How toxic is the pesticide for each route of potential overexposure — dermal (the pesticide falls on your skin and scalp while you're applying it), inhalation (you breathe in the spray or dust) or oral (you accidentally ingest the pesticide). In short, the question about natural pesticides isn't are they safer, but rather in which ways and for whom?

Debunking the Ads

The next step in assessing safety is debunking the popular belief that organic and natural are synonymous with safe and wholesome. All carbon compounds, including lab-synthesized pesticides, are classified as "organic." "Natural" pesticides, on the other hand, include only those products extracted from natural sources like plants. This is still no guarantee of safety. Many of the most poisonous chemicals known occur naturally.

CHERYL BEST *was an urban horticulture specialist with Cornell Cooperative Extension for eleven years and is now Director of Education at the Central Park Conservancy.*

Cutworm

Natural chemical pesticides, like synthetic chemical pesticides, can be potent poisons. Most natural pesticides do less ecological damage than synthetics because they break down rapidly when exposed to heat, light and water. This means they don't persist in the environment and are therefore unlikely to contaminate water and soil. "Residual effectiveness" is the specialist's term for a pesticide's ability to persist in its active toxic form for a relatively long time. Even the petrochemical-derived pesticides in wide use today generally have less residual effectiveness than now-banned pesticides like DDT which accumulated in the tissues of ospreys, eagles and other birds of prey and caused reproductive failure. However, residual effectiveness varies from pesticide to pesticide. The synthetic pesticide chlorpyrifos, which kills lawn and house pests, persists up to a year in soil, while glyphosate, an herbicide, is quickly inactivated in soil. Rotenone, a botanical pesticide used primarily on vegetable crops, breaks down quickly on plants and in soil and lasts up to a month in water, while ryania and pyrethrum last a relatively long time for botanicals.

Because natural pesticides have relatively low residual effectiveness, this might lead you to conclude that they are safe. But residual effectiveness is only one measure of safety. All pesticides are also rated according to their levels of acute toxicity: highly toxic, moderately toxic, slightly toxic and relatively nontoxic. This is represented by a value called an LD50 (meaning Lethal Dose: 50%). It is the single dose (in mg per kg of body weight) which when administered to laboratory test animals killed 50 percent of the population. LD50s are determined for oral exposure as well as inhalation and absorption through the skin. Because the numbers represent single doses, they cannot be used to determine chronic toxicity or non-lethal health effects. However, they are a valuable measure of the relative toxicity of chemicals. Pesticides containing chemicals with very high LD50s (5000mg/kg and above) are relatively nontoxic, whereas those containing chemicals with oral LD50s in the double digits (0 to 50mg/kg) can be highly toxic, depending on the formulation.

Natural pesticides can be derived from many sources. Five pesticides in common use today are botanicals, derived from plants. In order of lowest to highest LD50, these are: nicotine, rotenone, ryania, pyrethrum and sabadilla. The chart at right compares the LD50s of these botanicals with some popular synthetics.

Although all five botanicals break down relatively rapidly into harmless compounds once released in the environment, a few have other safety problems:

Nicotine, which is extracted from tobacco plants, is a violent poison that injures the human nervous system. It's also toxic to other mammals, as well as to birds and fish. Nicotine is particularly dangerous because it is a contact poison, meaning it is easily absorbed through the skin and does not have to be eaten to have toxic effects. A slightly less toxic formulation, nicotine sulfate, was once widely available, but its use is now restricted in many states. Pure nicotine is federally restricted and illegal for home gardeners nationwide. Nicotine sulfate, sold under the brand name Black Leaf 40, kills a broad range of sucking insects and larvae, including aphids and leaf miners. It also kills beneficial insects. If it's legal in your state and you decide to use it, wear protective clothing and apply with extreme caution.

Rotenone is extracted from the roots of many plants and is available as a 1 or 5 percent dust or wettable powder, or as a liquid formulated with other botanicals such as pyrethrum or ryania. The more compounds included, the broader its ability to kill and the higher its toxicity. Rotenone alone is approved by the U.S. Environmental Protection Agency (EPA) for

TOXICITY OF PESTICIDES
NATURAL AND SYNTHETIC

PESTICIDE	BOTANICAL/SYNTHETIC	ORAL LD50*	DERMAL LD50*
Rotenone	Botanical	50-75	>940
Nicotine Sulfate	Botanical	83	285
Propoxur	Synthetic	95-104	>1000
Chlorpyrifos	Synthetic	97-276	500-2,000
Diazinon	Synthetic	300-400	455-900
2,4-D	Synthetic	375-800	800-1,500
Carbaryl	Synthetic	500-850	>4,000
Ryania	Botanical	750-1,200	>4,000
Malathion	Synthetic	1,000-1,375	>4,444
Pyrethrum	Botanical	1,500	>1,880
Glyphosate	Synthetic	4,300	>7,940
Methoxychlor	Synthetic	5,000	>6,000
Sabadilla	Botanical	5,000	Little reaction
Benomyl	Synthetic	9,590	Little reaction

* An LD50 (Lethal Dose: 50%) is the single dose in mg per kg of body weight which, when administered to laboratory animals, killed 50% of them. LD50s are determined for oral exposure and absorption through the skin. Pesticides with very high LD50s (5,000 mg/kg and above) are relatively non-toxic. Pesticides containing chemicals with oral LD50s in the double digits (0 to 50 mg/kg) can be highly toxic, depending on the formulation.

Sod Webworm

use on a variety of edible and ornamental plants. It kills many insects, including Mexican bean beetles and flea beetles. It is most commonly available by its own name, but also by the trade names Prentox and Noxfish. The most powerful of the widely available botanicals, rotenone is moderately toxic to humans and many animals, and highly toxic to fish and other aquatic life. Therefore it should never be used near a waterway. Rotenone is both a stomach and a contact poison that slows the breathing and heart rates of many organisms, including mammals. Since rotenone is most commonly available as a dust, overexposure is most apt to occur through inhalation. Wear a protective mask while applying it.

Ryania is made by grinding up the stems of a South American shrub, *Ryania speciosa*. It doesn't kill insects outright but makes them too sick to eat the treated crop. Ryania is the most selective botanical pesticide, killing only a few pest species, including the European corn borer and coddling moth. Combination formulations like Triple Plus (Natur-Gro) kill a broader range of pests. Like rotenone, ryania is a contact and stomach poison available as a dust, but it is less toxic to mammals. However, it breaks down more slowly, so persists in the environment longer.

On crops, ryania should be applied long enough in advance of harvest to ensure that no residue remains on the food. This interval varies from crop to crop, but overall safe intervals are listed on the product label.

Gypsy Moth

Pyrethrum contains active ingredients called pyrethrins, which are extracted from the seeds of a species of chrysanthemum. It controls dozens of fruit and vegetable pests by paralyzing them on contact. Insects must be sprayed directly for the chemical to work, and will revive completely if they don't receive the lethal dose. For this reason, pyrethrum is often combined with rotenone in formulations such as Red Arrow Insect Spray. Some formulations contain the synthetic chemical synergist piperonyl butoxide for increased potency. Pyrethrum products are relatively non-toxic to humans but slightly toxic to fish and other aquatic life. Like rotenone, pyrethrum should not be used near waterways. Pyrethrins should not be confused with pyrethroids, synthetic compounds which break down more slowly in the environment and are more toxic to wildlife and honeybees.

Sabadilla comes from the seeds of a South American lily. These seeds contain toxic substances which rapidly decompose when exposed to light. Sabadilla is used to control lice, leafhoppers, squash bugs, striped cucumber beetles and chinch bugs. It's primarily a contact poison with low toxicity to wildlife. Usually formulated as a dust

Grasshopper

Gypsy Moth Larva

or wettable powder, Sabadilla is marketed by its own name and as Red Devil Dust. It is irritating to mucous membranes, so use a mask during application to protect your nose and throat. Sabadilla does have some residual effectiveness on plant surfaces, particularly when used in partial shade, but it breaks down more rapidly than ryania. Some studies indicate that it is toxic to bees; like other bee toxins, it should be applied during evening hours when honeybees generally are less active.

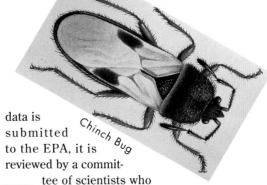

Chinch Bug

Whether you're using botanical or synthetic pesticides, clothing — long sleeves, pants, closed shoes and particularly hats (pesti-

White Grub

cides are most readily absorbed through the scalp) are a must. This clothing should be laundered separately, and after each use.

Rating Cancer Risks

When you think about the health effects of exposure to chemical pesticides, cancer is probably at the top of your list.

Fall Webworm

Unfortunately, there is no simple test that can determine definitively whether a pesticide does or doesn't cause cancer in humans.

Pesticides are rated for carcinogenicity (the capacity to cause cancer) by the EPA. The agency's ratings are based on years of long-term animal studies done by pesticide manufacturers themselves. Once the test data is submitted to the EPA, it is reviewed by a committee of scientists who then vote on the product's carcinogenicity rating. This is a complex task, because data on animals must be extrapolated to determine cancer risk to humans over a long period of exposure. The committee members do not always agree unanimously on the rating of a particular chemical. The final decision is by majority vote.

Rotenone, a botanical, is one pesticide on whose carcinogenicity rating committee members could not reach a consensus. Feeding studies did produce tumors in rats, but the majority ruled that rotenone is unlikely to cause cancer in humans.

Gardeners should also be aware of the fact that the EPA has not evaluated the carcinogenicity of many widely used pesticides. Only rotenone and two of the other pesticides listed on the accompanying chart have been evaluated for potential cancer risk — propoxur and benomyl, which are rated as probable and possible carcinogens, respectively. This is just one more reason why home gardeners should use pesticides — natural or synthetic — judiciously if at all. ⊕

Tent Caterpillar

This article is adapted from an article that appeared in Garbage *magazine.*

DESIGNING WITH NATURE IN NORTHERN NEW ENGLAND

BY PATRICK CHASSÉ

Nature is the ultimate garden master. Nature was the first owner of our gardens, and still exerts great influence over them. Recognizing this is the key to designing stable garden environments that require a minimum of maintenance. "Design with nature," as Ian McHarg put it in his 1969 book for planners, is also good advice for gardeners.

Nature is the main source of cues for the woodland gardens I design in northern New England. The East Asian tradition of emulating nature's forms and textures in a garden is a great inspiration. When the Chinese or Japanese talk about mountains and outcrops as the "bones of the earth," they are very much aware that, naked or green, it is these rocky "bones" which give the land its basic structure. Gardeners in the Far East study the most important elements of the natural landscape — the shape

PATRICK CHASSÉ *teaches landscape design at Radcliffe College and the Harvard Graduate School of Design. He is a principal of Landscape Design Associates, based in Northeast Harbor, Maine.*

and arrangement of landforms, the location and animation of water, the type and texture of stone, the patterns of vegetation, the relative scale of various elements — then distill them in a garden design. The smaller garden becomes a sort of visual echo of the larger natural setting and each complements the other.

Landforms

Designing a garden without regard for topography is like designing a stuffed toy without the filling. When designing gardens, the first thing I do is study the natural bones of the site and the surrounding countryside. I look at landforms: rounded or jagged? High or low? Soft or hard? Bold or subtle in texture? Then I think about how to recreate them on a smaller scale — what elements must be included to capture the essence of this landscape?

Here on the rockbound Maine coast, our bedrock underpinnings are very evident. The glaciated granite forms the foundation on which our forests, fields and wetlands grow, and it also determines the types and depths of soils that support these ecosystems. It provides not only the physical structure but also the aesthetic structure that gives them their visual character.

The character and placement of stone is of utmost importance in the natural garden. Whether I'm building or repairing a natural landscape, I try to replicate the natural pattern of stones. In some parts of New England that means mimicking rock outcrops. In other areas it means recreating a seemingly random distribution of weathered glacial boulders. If a garden in a stony area is devoid of stone, it will look out of place.

Soil

When the bones of a natural garden are in place, then the flesh should be added. Soil, which softens the topography and provides the medium for plant growth, should be chosen and placed with care. Again, it's critical to study the local soil — its pH, its texture, its nutrient content. All of these factors have helped determine which plant communities grow most comfortably in the area.

The success or failure of any natural garden is tied to how accurately the plants and the soils are matched. Soil pH is the factor most often overlooked. On the Maine coast, for example, the indigenous soils, derived mostly from granite and related rock types, are quite acidic. The high percentage of naturally occurring ericaceous plants in this area, such as lowbush blueberry, sheep laurel and mountain cranberry, need acid soil for best growth. By contrast, many monocots, including grasses, prefer a "sweeter" or more alkaline soil, which is why lawns in this area must be limed regularly. Using neutral or alkaline soils in a garden of local acid-loving woodland plants will work against you in two ways: The native plants will be less likely to thrive, and you'll be encouraging other species — especially grasses — which are highly aggressive weeds in the woodland plant community.

The idea is to have nature working with you rather than against you. If your soil and plantings don't match, you'll be forever weeding and nursing along your struggling native planting.

Light

The amount of light on site is another important consideration. I've often been called to a property whose owners longed for a lush native planting for a dense, light-starved patch of forest floor. This is particularly a problem when the tree canopy is primarily evergreen — as in Maine's spruce-fir forests. But it's also a problem in many older suburban gardens where evergreens such as hemlock or white pine, planted for privacy or to screen objectionable views, have matured into a dense tree canopy. The lack of light in these situations severely limits the choice of desirable plants.

If privacy is not the overriding consideration, a tree stand can be thinned to let in more light. But keep in mind that if you're trying to establish a native woodland planting, it's possible to introduce too much light, making conditions unfavorable for some desirable species — some ferns or mosses, for example. Within each of these plant groups normally considered shade tolerant there are species which can't tolerate strong light. For example, while hay-scented fern and haircap moss can thrive in full sun, male fern and cushion moss prefer low light. Too much light can also tip the balance in favor of the weeds. Again, grasses are often the invading villains when you're trying to establish a rich woodland ground flora and you introduce too much light.

Thinning branches from the top and sides of the tree canopy is a more subtle way to increase light than removing whole trees. It's much easier to remove a few more branches later than to try to replace a tree too hastily removed. To mask any hint of human intervention, thin and groom the

Blueberry ledges ablaze in autumn. Nature tends to plant in bold drifts.
So should natural landscapers.

overstory and the understory with studied irregularity. In too many woodland gardens the edge between groomed and untouched forest is as obvious as the edge between tall grass and a freshly mowed strip.

Plant Associations

Plants, of course, are a primary concern in gardening, wild or otherwise. There are two approaches to the planting composition of a natural garden: reproducing the natural associations of a native plant community, the mix and massing of species, using only native plants, or imitating the look of a natural plant community, using a variety of plants both exotic and native. The latter has been the inspiration for many gardens here and abroad — particularly for the classic English rhododendron garden with its exotic shrub and ground cover collections planted as nat-

"Native sod" rescued from a blueberry farm, including white-flowered bunchberry dogwood.

It's difficult to tell which rock outcrops are natural and which are not.

In this garden the author exposed the natural rock ledge and
used matching stone to create a patio.

NATIVE PLANTS FOR NORTHEAST WOODLAND GARDENS

Acer pensylvanicum	Moose maple
Amelanchier canadensis	Shadbush
Amelanchier laevis	Shadbush
Aralia hispida	Bristly sarsaparilla
Aralia nudicaulis	Wild sarsaparilla
Arctostaphylos uva-ursi	Bearberry
Asarum canadense	Wild ginger
Aster macrophyllus	Bigleaf aster
Clintonia borealis	Bluebead lily
Comptonia peregrina	Sweet fern
Cornus canadensis	Bunchberry dogwood
Dennstaedtia punctilobula	Hay-scented fern
Dryopteris filix-mas	Male fern
Thelypteris noveboracensis	New York fern
Gaultheria procumbens	Wintergreen
Gaylussacia baccata	Huckleberry
Ilex verticillata	Winterberry
Kalmia angustifolia	Sheep laurel
Maianthemum canadense	Wild lily-of-the-valley
Myrica pensylvanica	Bayberry
Osmunda cinnamomea	Cinnamon fern
Polypodium virginianum	Rock fern
Polystichum acrostichoides	Christmas fern
Polytrichum commune	Haircap moss
Rosa virginiana	Virginia rose
Thalictrum polygamum	Meadow rue
Trientalis borealis	Starflower
Vaccinium angustifolium	Lowbush blueberry
Vaccinium corymbosum	Highbush blueberry
Vaccinium vitis-idaea	Mountain cranberry
Viburnum alnifolium	Hobblebush
Viburnum cassinoides	Wild raisin
Viburnum dentatum	Arrowwood
Viola spp.	Violets

uralized woodland understories.

Natural landscaping based on native plant communities is more of an American idea, closely allied with our appreciation of wilderness. But this type of ecologically naturalistic garden is far more difficult to plant because many native species are not yet available in the nursery trade and collecting them from the wild can endanger sparse populations. The difficulty of finding the plants you want becomes an important design consideration. I usually tailor the design of my wild gardens to the list of what is readily available.

Many of the native North American plants propagated for sale in nurseries are woody plants, and many have been on ornamental plant lists since the 17th and 18th centuries. Long-time nursery favorites like mountain laurel and paper birch were introduced from North America into European gardens before the American Revolution. These American plant celebrities are still popular, but their cousins sheep laurel and yellow birch still aren't widely appreciated or sold. Other plants — trilliums, for example — are available at nurseries but too frequently are dug from the wild and then potted up for sale, threatening native populations. Often, plants that grow in bold masses in the wild are the most common native plants in an area, and the hardiest. Fortunately, these plants also tend to have great visual impact — both in nature and when massed in the garden. When these species are available at nurseries, it's a safe bet that they can be used in the natural garden without endangering plant populations.

In addition to nursery stock we use plants from three "wild" sources: from elsewhere on the garden site, from "rescue" sites (that is, construction or agricultural sites where the plants are earmarked for destruction) and from private property — with permission, of course. Rescue sites are my favorite. Our richest rescue source is the thousands of acres of blueberry fields in eastern Maine. Lowbush blueberries are marketed as "wild blueberries" but the fields are actually groomed, burned and treated with chemical sprays. Because some of the most pernicious weeds are ericaceous like the blueberries themselves, herbicides which might control them are toxic to the blueberries. Patches of these woody weeds are tolerated until they're so large that it makes sense to plow them up and replace them with crop stock. It just happens that among these "weeds" are bunchberry dogwood, wintergreen, haircap moss and hay-scented fern — all beautiful plants for natural woodland gardens in northern New England. Our biggest windfall in the last few years came from a large field about to be cleared to make a playing field at a local private school. We cut the plants with a sod cutter and moved them out before the bulldozers moved in. Development in natural areas is a controversial issue. But when destruction is inevitable, it's satisfying to be able to save at least some of the native flora.

Once you've chosen a plant community and located the plants, design of a natural garden is similar to that of conventional ornamental plantings. Now the aesthetics of the arrangement is your primary concern — massing, scale, color, texture, seasonal change. Unless you have an eye for the rare and tend to find inconspicuous plants the most interesting, you're probably most attracted to the more dramatic beauty of masses of plants in nature. Nature tends to paint in bold strokes. Unless I'm deliberately using a plant as an accent, I never plant in groups of fewer than three, and often plant by the dozens. I arrange each mass in relation to its neighbors, usually in incremental steps from ground cover up through understory, shrub and tree layers. I also plant for changing color and texture through the seasons. Brilliant red blueberry and huckleberry and yellow moosewood foliage become a highlight in autumn after a season as a green backdrop, while fruits and twigs of bayberry and winterberry liven up the winter months.

Edges

Connecting the planting to the surrounding landscape is an element of wild garden design that can't be stressed enough. Plant communities in nature blend in characteristic ways. A common plant association in New England is a meadow edged by shrubs which blend into the understory of a forest.

There are few clear-cut edges, unless there is also an underlying radical change in soils or moisture conditions. When planting out into a natural setting, or creating an entire plant community, gardeners too often end the planting as they would a herbaceous border — with a nice tidy line. Instead, try making the density of the planting more open as you move to the perimeter with a few small "islands" of plants floating out into the mostly unplanted ground. The same goes for clearing the forest understory: Where the weed wacker or pruning saw stopped shouldn't be obvious to the eye.

Planting

One thing to keep in mind when you get down to the actual planting of a woodland garden is that the plants will often be sparse — usually because you have used young plant stock — and it's important to discourage weeds by mulching thoroughly. Look at the model plant community for clues about what to use as mulch. If oak leaves, for example, or pine needles are the naturally occuring mulch, use them in your garden. (When was the last time you saw bark chips the size of barbecue briquettes covering the forest floor?) Another thing to keep in mind is the pH of the mulch and its effect on the soil.

Don't fertilize when you plant! The soils that support many wild plant communities are relatively low in fertility. A big shot of nitrogen might benefit the weeds more than the desired plants. You can always add nutrients later, when there is clear evidence that something is in short supply.

Maintenance

Here are a few rules of thumb for maintenance of newly established native woodland gardens:

◆ During the first full season, water whenever soil moisture falls below ideal levels for the new plants. If your plants have been properly matched, they should have similar moisture requirements. When the planting is well established it should require no additional watering, except during severe drought.

◆ Weed frequently. The bigger the weeds, the more they will disturb the soil when pulled. If you don't weed diligently the first year, you may lose control of the planting and not be able to wrest it back from the intruders. Indeed, the first three years are critical.

◆ Keep bare soil between plants well mulched to discourage weeds and conserve moisture. Check and loosen mulch regularly to allow rhizomatous and stoloniferous plants to spread. Don't use plastic sheeting. One way to keep costs down is by using a heavy "working mulch" (such as shredded bark) with an attractive "dress mulch" (such as pine needles) on top.

◆ Don't be concerned if there isn't much leaf growth at first. Even if vegetative growth is slow during the first season, the roots may be actively establishing themselves.

◆ Check the soil pH after the first winter and adjust if necessary. If there has been a dramatic change (0.5 or more), keep checking and amending the soil regularly. ⊕

HOW TO CREATE
A STREAMSIDE GARDEN
INCLUDING THE STREAM

BY DAVID B. MELCHERT

During the past century and a half, wildlife habitats in this country have changed dramatically. Forests have been cleared, prairies plowed, marshes drained and streams diverted. Some wildlife species, such as blue jays and robins, have been able to take advantage of these changes and increase their ranges. Others, like the spotted owl and northern parula, have responded to their ever-shrinking habitat by declining drastically in numbers or, worse, becoming extinct.

As gardeners we have the opportunity, and the ability, to offset the increasing loss of wildlife habitat. One of the more productive habitats that can be incorporated in a garden is a streamside habitat. The inclusion of water, even in the smallest setting, will vastly increase the number — and perhaps the variety — of species that frequent an area.

DAVID B. MELCHERT *is a landscape architect and founding partner at the Stroudwater Design Group in Portland, Maine. His work has included master plans and landscape designs for homes, college campuses and parks with native plantings and habitat restorations.*

Streams are common in many natural settings, from deep forests to open fields. They provide a wide variety of habitat features, including moss-covered rocks that provide cover for salamanders and insects and deep water for large fish and birds. Given this diversity of natural settings and habitat features, a streamside garden is appropriate in almost any garden setting.

Planning Your Garden

Your streamside garden should include aquatic, riparian (along the banks) and upland (either woodland or meadow) habitats. Below are some basic considerations that will determine which kinds of habitat improvements you should make:

Special habitat features. The success of your streamside garden will depend on its ability to provide for the specific needs of wildlife common to your area. For example, many salamanders, including the spotted salamander, need proper water pH to reproduce and logs and rocks for cover. The sedge wren is dependent upon sedge meadows of cordgrass (*Spartina patens*), while the yellow-rumped warbler needs spruces and hemlocks for summer breeding and

STREAMSIDE GARDEN FLORA & FAUNA

The following is a list of plants for streamside gardens
and the wildlife they're likely to attract.

CANOPY TREES

American beech (*Fagus grandiflora*)	Wood duck, ruffed grouse, tufted titmouse, fox squirrel, Eastern chipmunk
Balsam fir (*Abies balsamea*)	Nuthatch, chickadee, red squirrel, porcupine, white-tailed deer, moose
Birch (*Betula* spp.)	Ruffed grouse, common redpoll, black-capped chickadee, pine siskin, beaver, cottontail, white-tailed deer, moose
Eastern hemlock (*Tsuga canadensis*)	Pine siskin, white-winged crossbill, chickadee, porcupine, red squirrel, deer
Maple (*Acer* spp.)	Grouse, bobwhite, evening grosbeak, red-breasted nuthatch, porcupine, fox squirrel, chipmunk
Red oak (*Quercus rubrum*)	Wood duck, bobwhite, wild turkey, grackle, blue jay, white-breasted nuthatch, brown thrasher, titmouse, red-eyed towhee, racoon, red and gray squirrel, deer
White pine (*Pinus strobus*)	Mourning dove, chickadee, red crossbill, pine grosbeak, red-breasted nuthatch, pine siskin, pine warbler, Eastern cottontail, gray squirrel, chipmunk, white-footed mouse

bayberry thickets for winter foraging. Before you can create the special habitat conditions that will attract wildlife, you must learn about the species native to your area and their needs.

For aquatic wildlife you'll need to consider the type of stream bottom, the variability of water flow, the average depth of the water and the water temperature and pH. For plants and animals associated with the riparian and upland habitats, special needs include the forest type, plant associations, the vertical structure of the vegetation, the size of existing live and dead trees, the amount of shade and the quality of the duff layer — the natural layer of soil, leaves and twigs on the forest floor. These features can be woven into your garden's design along with such traditional considerations as proper scale, color and texture.

The size of your garden. All animals require a certain size habitat for feeding, nesting and mating. The size varies with each species; a leopard frog requires only 25

UNDERCANOPY TREES

Mountain ash (*Sorbus aucuparia*) — Grouse, pine grosbeak, olive-backed thrush, cedar waxwing, purple finch

Pin cherry (*Prunus pensylvanica*) — Grouse, ring-necked pheasant, evening and rose-breasted grosbeak, blue jay, oriole, mockingbird, robin, brown thrasher, gray-checked thrush, waxwing, pileated woodpecker, red fox, opossum, rabbit, racoon, gray squirrel, chipmunk, moose

Shadblow (*Amelanchier canadensis*) — Grouse, Eastern bluebird, cardinal, catbird, crow, blue jay, oriole, mockingbird, robin, scarlet tanager, brown thrasher, hermit thrush, downy woodpecker, skunk, red squirrel

Speckled alder (*Alnus rugosa*) — Goldfinch, common redpoll, pine siskin, beaver, hare, moose

Sumac (*Rhus* spp.) — Grouse, turkey, bluebird, cardinal, catbird, purple finch, junco, mockingbird, phoebe, robin, scarlet tanager, hermit thrush, warbling vireo, cottontail, deer

White cedar (*Thuja occidentalis*) — Purple finch, bluebird, pine grosbeak, cedar waxwing, meadow mouse, deer

Continued on page 50

to 100 square meters of habitat, for instance, whereas neotropical migrants such as warblers often require forested areas of more than twelve acres. Thus, the size of your garden will determine the types of wildlife that will visit, and this in turn should govern the specific kinds of habitat that you create.

In general, large gardens will provide habitat opportunities for a greater diversity of wildlife and for larger animals than small gardens. If your garden is large, take advantage of this opportunity and model it closely after native plant communities to create the best habitat possible.

Whether your garden is large or small, you can "enlarge" it by "borrowing" from a nearby park or natural area. With its linear nature, a streamside garden will function quite nicely as a vegetated corridor which wildlife will use to travel from one area to another. In any case, if your garden can compensate for some scarcity of habitat in your area, its attractiveness to wildlife will be greatly enhanced. The inclusion of water is often such a major attraction.

The source of water for your stream. In this age of pumps and man-made liners, it's possible to have a streamside garden almost anywhere. Keep in mind, though, that a man-made stream can be costly to construct and maintain. What's more, some synthetic liners are toxic to fish and other aquatic animals. Consult the manufacturer before you buy.

A natural source of water is preferable to domestic water, which passes through copper or galvanized pipes and is often chlorinated and thus is harmful to fish and other aquatic life. As an alternative, you can take advantage of natural water flow by channeling it into a small ditch or swale. You can reopen a culverted stream. Or you can make minor improvements to an existing wet area or stream channel to create productive habitat that previously did not exist.

Whether water is provided by mechanical or natural means, the type of aquatic habitat you'll be able to create will be determined largely by the consistency of water flow within the stream channel. Intermittent or seasonal water flows make for different kinds of habitat than streams with relatively stable water flows and levels.

A backyard stream needn't have a high level of water to be productive habitat. An intermittent stream, with low water flows, provides important habitat for insects, amphibians and reptiles, in addition to sources of food and water for migrating birds. An intermittent stream can easily be included in most gardens, even small ones. Larger gardens can have more active streams that sustain larger fish, birds and mammals as well.

Water quality. The chemical and physical properties of water play an important role in healthy aquatic environments. For example, fish and salamanders are sensitive to the pH of stream water. You may need to test the water if you want to attract certain species of wildlife. In general, though, most natural water sources will be acceptable.

Clear water is also important. Natural sources of water may have silt- and nutrient-laden runoff which hinders light penetration. If this is a problem, you can construct a settling pool or small wetland upstream with plants such as cattails (*Typha* spp.), bulrushes (*Scirpus* spp.) and sedges (*Carex* spp.) to help remove silt and nutrients from the water.

Vegetative buffers along the banks of the stream will also protect water quality. Plants with fibrous roots such as red-twig dogwood (*Cornus sericea*) and winterberry (*Ilex verticillata*) will control erosion. Maintaining the duff layer along the stream bank is also extremely important because it will absorb nutrient runoff and silt before they

This stream restoration designed by the author for a home in Maine includes small dams created by developing ledge banks across the width of the stream channel, with "plunge pools" below.

enter the stream. Never replace the natural duff layer with commercial mulch.

Creating Your Streamside Garden

Although our gardens can never fully replace pristine native habitat, they can provide basic food, cover and nesting requirements. The following guidelines will help you create the basic elements of aquatic, riparian and upland habitat in your streamside garden.

Building the Stream

Stream channels operate in a consistent, self-maintaining manner which has been perfected over time until an equilibrium is reached and the channel and its banks become relatively stable. Changes in the physical structure of an existing stream channel will result in a series of downstream adjustments until a new equilibrium is reached. In other words, if you're not careful, your physical habitat "improvements" can actually result in a decrease in habitat quality. Several aspects of stream mechanics — the configuration of the stream channel, width/depth ratios, gradient, stream bank structure and sediment loading — are critical for a healthy stream environment but go beyond the scope of this article. Consult a professional before altering an existing stream channel. To create a new stream, you'll need a basic understanding of stream morphology.

Before you start, study natural streams in your area. Pay special attention to patterns of stream flow, bank forms and bottom materials of streams similar to the type you want to create in your garden. Here are some things to consider when you develop the stream itself:

Stream profile. The profile of your stream channel should provide a number of different habitat opportunities. There should be areas of shallower, faster moving water (riffles) as well as areas with calmer, deeper water (guides) and occasional pools. Include wetland areas to accommodate any flooding that may occur. The wetlands will also provide some of the most productive habitat along your stream.

Water depth. Water depth determines which plant associations are appropriate, provides safety from predators and regulates temperatures within the stream. Try to vary the depth of your stream to provide habitat for as many species as possible.

As you're laying out your stream and selecting the plants, keep in mind that certain plant species grow only within a given range of depths. Plants such as duck corn (*Peltandra virginica*) prosper in swampy areas to water depths of one foot, while wild celery (*Vallisneria spiralis*) will grow in

ILLUSTRATIONS BY STROUDWATER DESIGN GROUP

STREAMSIDE GARDEN FLORA & FAUNA

SHRUBS

Bayberry (*Myrica pensylvanica*)	Yellow dowitcher, grouse, bluebird, catbird, chickadee, meadowlark, tree swallow, towhee, scarlet tanager
Blueberry (*Vaccinium corymbosum*)	Herring gull, grouse, bluebird, catbird, yellow-breasted chat, chickadee, crested flycatcher, blue jay, oriole, phoebe, tree sparrow, scarlet tanager, red fox, opossum, Eastern skunk, chipmunk, red-backed mouse, deer
Canadian rhodora (*Rhodora canadense*)	Hummingbirds, butterflies, bees
Elderberry (*Sambucus canadensis*)	Pheasant, rusty blackbird, bluebird, indigo bunting, cardinal, catbird, yellow-breasted chat, rose-breasted grosbeak, Eastern kingbird, phoebe, robin, swamp, white-crowned and white-throated sparrow, scarlet tanager, tufted titmouse, veery, wood thrush, waxwing, red squirrel, woodchuck, white-footed mouse, moose

depths of one-and-a-half to ten feet.

Stream banks. Stream banks should be stable and have ample room for plantings. They should fit in with the existing topography and look natural. In well defined channels you can include stabilized "cuts" under the bank to provide cover for fish and other aquatic animals (see the illustration on the bottom of the next page). In cool climates, bank cover can extend into areas of slower-moving water to create bog-like conditions. Over time, peat will accumulate and a floating mat of vegetation, commonly sundew (*Drosera* spp.) and pitcher plant (*Sarracenia* spp.), will form. You should also provide access to the water with either a sand bar, ledge or fallen tree, so that animals will be able to drink and bathe. Be careful not to create a sudden drop-off in these areas.

Stream bottom. How do you decide what kind of bottom materials are best for your stream? This will depend on the rate of water flow and the needs of wildlife you're trying to attract. Several types of bottom usually exist in the same stream.

BEDROCK bottoms occur where there is natural ledge. When there is no natural ledge, it's possible to simulate it along the bank or stream bottom to control erosion and provide access to the water for wildlife. Low- and medium-height "dams" along the

Huckleberry (*Gaylussacia* spp.)	Grouse, white-winged crossbill, pine grosbeak, scarlet tanager, red-eyed towhee, deer
Mountain laurel (*Kalmia latifolia*)	Grouse, deer
Raspberry (*Rubus* spp.)	Grouse, bobwhite, cardinal, catbird, yellow-breasted chat, pine grosbeak, blue jay, oriole, robin, Henslow sparrow, titmouse, red-eyed towhee, waxwing, black bear, fox, red squirrel, chipmunk, white-footed mouse, deer, moose
Snowberry (*Symphoricarpo*s spp.)	Grouse, pheasant, purple finch, pine grosbeak, hummingbird, robin, hermit thrush, hare, deer
Swamp azalea (*Rhododendron viscosum*)	Hummingbird, butterflies, bees
Viburnum (*Viburnum* spp.)	Grouse, cardinal, robin, gray-cheeked thrush, waxwing, cottontail, skunk, Eastern chipmunk, white-footed mouse
Winterberry (*Ilex verticillata*)	Black duck, grouse, bluebird, catbird, mockingbird, robin, wood thrush, towhee, cedar waxwing, pileated woodpecker

Continued on page 54

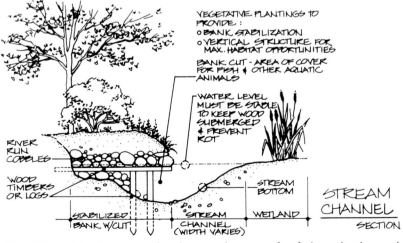

Stabilized "cuts" in the streambank provide cover for fish and other wildlife.

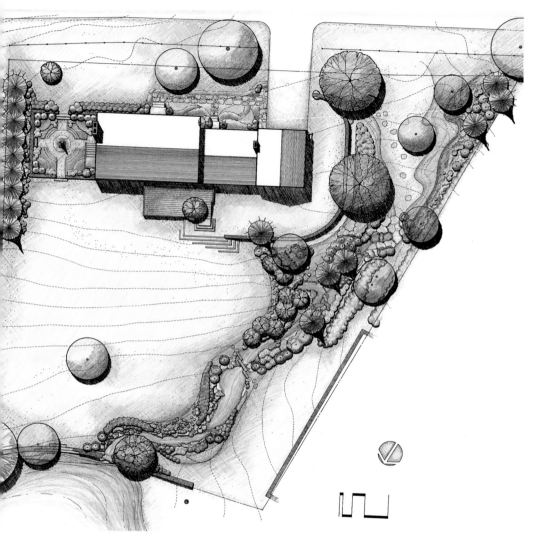

This landscape plan includes the restoration of a stream which had been diverted into a culvert and bulldozed when the home was built.

stream can be developed by creating ledge banks across the width of the stream channel. Below these dams "plunge pools" form, providing cover for fish and increasing the level of oxygen in the water. They also provide pleasant sounds as water rushes across the ledge and tumbles into the pool.

BOULDERS placed in riffles and guides provide cover for fish traveling between pools.

Water velocity increases as the water goes around the rock, creating a "scour pool" at its base where fish can hide. How big the boulders should be depends upon how fast the water flows; the faster the flow, the larger the stones. A general rule of thumb is to use stones two to three feet in diameter.

COBBLES are large rocks, six to eighteen inches in diameter, typically associated with

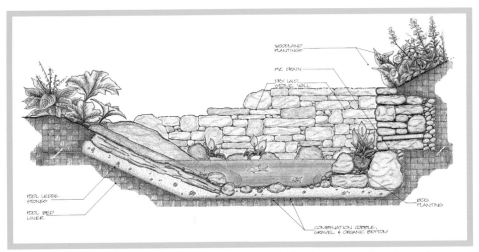

Even a tiny garden can include a natural-looking woodland pool.

faster-moving water. They provide cover for small fish, insects, crustaceans and amphibians. Cobbles are also useful in controlling erosion and stabilizing streambanks.

GRAVEL provides cover and spawning ground for fish, insects, amphibians and other animals. To spawn, trout and salmon require riffles with an area of clean gravel at least two feet square. Gravel bottoms are common in areas of mild flow and in intermittent streams.

SAND is common on the inside edges of pools where the water slows and particles are deposited. Guides with slower-moving water often have sand bottoms, as do intermittent streams.

MUD bottoms are common in slower-moving waters that traverse fine-textured soils. They provide habitat for reptiles, amphibians, crustaceans, insects and some warm-water fish. Plants readily grow in this type of stream bottom. Consequently, mud bottoms are one of the more productive habitat areas in a streamside garden.

ORGANIC bottoms occur where substantial amounts of leaves or other organic material are deposited. They typically develop in areas where the flushing rate is low. Fallen wood, leaves and other stream litter provide food and cover for wildlife, and to some extent influence the acidity of the water and add important trace minerals. A properly placed log or decaying leaves will provide habitat for insects, crustaceans, fish, amphibians and frogs. They in turn will attract birds and other predators.

By randomly mixing areas of different depth, water flow and bottom materials in your stream, you can create habitats for a number of plants and animals. The illustration on page 55 shows how these elements can be combined in a stream.

Selecting the Plants

Plant selection for your streamside habitat should be guided not only by your garden's location and the types of plants that grow there, but also by the needs of the wildlife you wish to attract. It can't be stressed enough that to attract the greatest number and diversity of wildlife, you need to recreate native plant associations as closely as possible. If your garden can compensate for any kind of habitat scarcity in your area, such as a food source or shelter in places with bitter winters, you'll greatly boost your garden's ability to attract wildlife. Develop a plant palette that provides for the needs of both permanent residents and temporary visitors. The essential

STREAMSIDE GARDEN FLORA & FAUNA

GROUND COVERS

Bearberry (*Arctostaphylos uva-ursi*) — Grouse, deer

Bunchberry (*Cornus canadensis*) — Ipswich sparrow, veery thrush, Philadelphia vireo, warbling vireo

Christmas fern (*Polystichum acrostichoides*) — Ruffed grouse, hare, white-tailed deer

Mosses — Trumpeter swan, lemming mouse

Wintergreen (*Gaultheria procumbens*) — Grouse, white-footed mouse, white-tailed deer

Partridgeberry (*Mitchella repens*) — Grouse, bobwhite, red fox, white-footed mouse

AQUATIC AND EMERGENT PLANTS

Pickerel plant (*Pontederia cordata*) — Black duck, wood duck, muskrat

Wapato (*Sagittaria latifolia*) — Black duck, canvasback, mallard, lesser scaup, wood duck, muskrat

Wild celery (*Vallisneria spiralis*) — Coot, black duck, canvasback, mallard, American goldeneye, redhead duck

Wild rice (*Zizania aquatica*) — Coot, black duck, bufflehead, pintail, teal, wood duck, redwing blackbird, bobolink, song sparrow

---

elements of any productive habitat are food, shelter and a place to raise young.

Food. The plants in your streamside garden should provide a broad spectrum of foods for a variety of wildlife. Consider plants not only for the obvious sources of food they provide (fleshy fruits, tubers, nuts and seeds) but also for the "secondary" types of food they attract (insects, snails, fish and other small animals). The tender shoots, buds and seed pods of wild celery are an important food for diving and marsh ducks and provide food and cover for snails, minute insects, plankton and other aquatic life. Other animals will come to feed on these secondary sources of food. Warblers will be attracted to plantings of maples, alders, birches, dogwoods, hawthorns, oaks and buckthorns, which are good insect-attracting plants. If possible, include dead trees, or snags, in your garden, which are an important source of insects for wildlife.

Shelter and cover. Plants provide shelter from the weather and cover from predators. They offer relief from the midday sun, a place to roost for the night and a refuge from soaking rain, biting wind or freezing cold. In cold climates evergreen trees and shrubs are a must for wildlife which remain for the winter. Thickets and tangles of hawthorn, native roses such as *Rosa virginiana*, *R. carolina* and *R. palustris* and barberry offer good protection from predators.

Nesting. Generally, if you include a variety of evergreen and deciduous plants of different heights, wildlife will be able to nest. You can supplement nesting opportunities with brush piles and houses for birds and bats. Dead trees will also provide places for owls, woodpeckers and other species to nest.

Plant associations. Individual species of wildlife have developed specific relationships with plants that provide the foraging and nesting opportunities they need. Species like the northern parula need bogs with hundred-foot-high conifers that have bearded lichen (*Usnea*) for nesting, as well as a deciduous undercanopy for gleaning insects. The Nashville warbler requires moist, open deciduous habitats with moss-covered depressions or dense ferneries for nesting. The Cape May warbler prefers dense spruce-fir forests typically thirty to sixty feet in height. These kinds of species/habitat associations are often disrupted when a natural area becomes a patchwork of urban or suburban gardens. For this reason your stream-side garden will be most successful as wildlife habitat if you base it as closely as possible on plant associations native to your area. Such associations include a mix of canopy and undercanopy trees, shrubs, ground covers, forbs, grasses and emergent and floating vegetation.

Vertical structure. Developing the vertical structure of your plantings is an important part of habitat creation. Simply put, this means recreating the layered effect of natural vegetation — from the crowns of canopy trees down to the ground covers on the forest floor. Look at the woodlands in your area: Are they canopy woods only or are there one or two intermediate layers of vegetation, such as undercanopy trees and shrubs? The vertical structure of vegetation is important because different species favor different layers for different needs. Northern orioles, for instance, nest in the canopies of tall deciduous trees like maples and forage for food in understory fruit trees and berry patches.

For suggestions on plants for your streamside garden, see the list which begins on page 46. The illustrations on pages 48 and 53 show how all the different elements can be brought together in your garden. ⊕

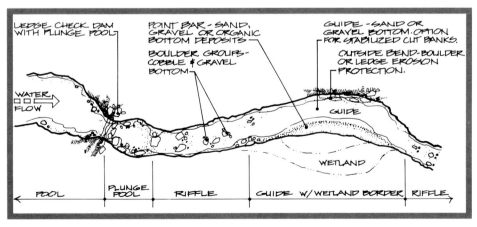

In your stream, try to randomly mix areas of different depth, water flow and bottom materials.

MEADOWS AND HEDGEROWS

BY EDMUND HOLLANDER
AND MARYANNE CONNELLY

Planting meadows and hedgerows, especially on subdivided farmland, is a wonderful way to preserve the historic agricultural landscape.

Meadows and hedgerows are easy on the environment—and easy to maintain—because they work with natural succession. Hedgerows provide privacy from neighbors and habitat for wildlife.

More and more of our clients are turning away from endless stretches of lawn and clipped hedges of privet and yew. They want wildflower meadows and hedgerows instead.

As recently as fifty or sixty years ago, meadow and pasture bordered by dense,

---

EDMUND HOLLANDER *is president of Edmund Hollander Design, a New York firm which includes environmental planners, landscape architects and horticulturists. He has designed natural landscapes throughout the Northeast and teaches landscape architecture at the University of Pennsylvania.*
MARYANNE CONNELLY *is a landscape architect who has worked on a variety of projects in the New York metropolitan area and teaches at the New York Botanical Garden.*

linear hedgerows was the landscape pattern that dominated the Northeast. Indeed, it's a pattern that dates back to colonial times in the United States and all the way back to the Middle Ages in Britain. Suburban sprawl has obliterated much of our traditional agricultural landscape. Whenever we design a home garden, a horse farm or even a corporate headquarters on newly subdivided farmland, we try to incorporate meadows and hedgerows. It's a wonderful way to preserve the historic agricultural landscape.

When farmland on what was originally forest is released from the rigorous agricultural regimen, it goes through a natural process called succession, with local variations. Understanding this process is critical to the successful establishment of a meadow. Millions of seeds lay dormant in the soil. When the soil is exposed and they are able to germinate, there is an explosion of physiologically tough, aggressive annuals like horseweed and common ragweed. In a few years, biennials, many alien species like common mullein and Queen Anne's lace, move in, along with a few wildflowers like asters (*Aster* spp.) and goldenrods (*Solidago* spp.) After five years or so, the meadow is in full bloom with native and naturalized species such as ox-eye daisy (*Chrysanthemum leucanthemum*), black-eyed susan (*Rudbeckia hirta*) and butterfly weed (*Asclepias tuberosa*) complementing the biennials and interspersed with big bluestem (*Andropogon gerardii*), little bluestem (*Schizachyrium scoparium*) and switch grass (*Panicum virgatum*). Within a few years seedlings of maple, ash, dogwood, cherry, crabapple, pine and cedar grow up and rapidly transform the meadow into "old field." This is an extremely rich, floriferous blend of trees, shrubs and herbaceous species particularly favored by wildlife. As the canopy trees mature they shade out the grasses, wildflowers, evergreens and shrubs and the land reverts back to woodland from whence it came.

Hedgerows grew up between fields or pastures, usually around fences or stone walls. Mature hedgerows typically included tall canopy species like ash, maple and oak along with understory trees like dogwood, hawthorn and cherry and shrubs such as viburnum, sumac and rose. Wildflowers and grasses bordered the field. Songbirds flourish in this environment, which is a carpet of flowers in spring and a cornucopia of fruits and nuts in fall and winter. This attractive habitat is not only an important food source and migration corridor for wildlife, but also a seed bank for future woodlands.

Planting a Meadow

A successful meadow requires some research. Look to see what's growing in fields around you; particular soil conditions and microclimates determine the individual species that are best adapted to your area. These should form the basis of your seed mix. While meadows should consist predominantly of plants native to your area, there are no hard and fast rules, and individual favorites usually can be accommodated. Ox-eye daisy will seed itself in, but shasta and other daisies are appropriate as well. After all, natural succession creates meadows which are colorful and exuberant mixtures of both native and exotic species — a kind of ecological melting pot.

The bulk of your meadow should be perennials, plants that come back year after year. Stay away from many commercial "meadow in a can" mixes, which are largely annuals. They'll give a good show the first year, but after that usually require reseeding. Some annuals, perhaps 20 percent, should be part of your seed mix, along with clump grasses like *Andropogon* and *Panicum*.

Another important part of establishing a meadow is preparing the seed bed. Remember, if succession had its way, your meadow would be filled with six-foot-tall ragweed right off the bat. If you have time and patience, you can let nature take its course. What we try to do is skip the first five to seven years of succession, go straight to the "perennial" stage and keep it that way. This can be done mechanically or chemically, but we prefer the mechanical approach. First, cut all the existing vegetation down to a height of three to four inches. Then disk, harrow or rototill the ground to break up the sods and turn under the existing vegetation. Wait several weeks for the seeds in the soil to germinate and then turn them under again. Next, rake the soil lightly to prepare a loose, friable seed bed while creating as little disturbance as possible. Then spread the seed at approximately one half pound per 1,000 square feet. Roll or tamp the seed into the soil to make sure there is good contact and water lightly yet thoroughly.

After watering, add a straw mulch. Wildflower seedlings are as tender and fragile as any other plant. If they germinate and then dry out, they'll die. If you plant in early spring or early fall, there's a good chance that there will be enough rainfall. Be prepared, though, to provide additional water if necessary. After the seeds germinate it's critical to provide them with sufficient moisture.

Your meadow will, in most cases, require some maintenance the first year or two. It's a good idea to remove any unwanted plants like ragweed as soon as they are recognizable. These very aggressive annuals will compete for water and space and can shade out the slower-growing perennials. One solution we've found is to wait until mid-June when the annuals are much taller than the perennials. At that point we either mow or hand cut all the plants above the top height of the wildflowers — usually about twelve inches. This prevents the annuals from going to seed but saves us the trouble of having to pull them out by hand. Once your meadow is established, all that will be required is an annual mowing in late fall to discourage any woody seedlings that have taken hold and aid seed dispersal.

If you have a small yard you can either skip the seeding process entirely or supplement it with container- or field-grown perennial wildflowers planted in the clump and gap patterns typically found in this type of plant association. Wildflower sods are also available.

Planting a Hedgerow

Planting a hedgerow is somewhat simpler, although more expensive and labor intensive. Hedgerows as well as meadows should consist of mostly native species, but you needn't take a purist approach. While the wild crabapple (*Malus coronaria*) is found naturally in a hedgerow, a variety of crabapple cultivars — 'Snowdrift', 'Zumi' and 'Floribunda', for example — can be planted in a new hedgerow. As with the meadow, look and see what's growing in your area. Have the soil tested. Find out if the soil is sandy or heavy with clay, well drained or soggy, acidic or alkaline. Deer browsing may also need to be taken into consideration. Then choose your plants accordingly.

Plant the center or tallest part of the hedgerow with maple, ash, oak, tulip and other canopy trees which grow in your area. We like to plant the more natural clump forms rather than the standard shade tree forms. On either side and among the taller species, plant both flowering and evergreen trees. We typically plant crabapple (*Malus*), hawthorn (*Crataegus*), dogwood (*Cornus*) and cherry (*Prunus*) for both their flowers and fruits. Either red cedar (*Juniperus virginiana*) or white pine (*Pinus strobus*) add an evergreen component to the hedgerow. After the trees are installed you can plant any number of shrubs on the outside edges, including viburnums (*Viburnum* spp.), bayberry (*Myrica pensylvanica*), species roses, shrub dogwoods and sumac (*Rhus* spp.). There really is a great deal of flexibility as far as what will grow in a hedgerow.

Your reason for planting the hedgerow will also influence what species and sizes you include. If privacy is your main goal, include more evergreens. If you're planting primarily for wildlife, include oaks (*Quercus* spp.), hickories (*Carya* spp.) and beeches (*Fagus* spp.) as canopy trees as well as flowering trees and shrubs that provide fruit over an extended period.

The beauty of the hedgerow and meadow is that they work with natural systems. They can accomplish numerous design goals. They can include native species as well as personal favorites. And after some initial care they require very little work — in return for a great deal of beauty. ⊕

NATIVE GARDENS FOR METROPOLITAN NEW YORK

BY Steven Clemants

Dune grass, bayberry, bearberry and scrub oak
grow among the dunes in Napeague, Long Island.

Metropolitan New York has many habitats, from broad sandy plains to gneiss and granite outcrops to concrete pavements. What's more, the region spans three hardiness zones. Within this mix of geology and climate many different plant communities have evolved. This great diversity presents endless opportunities for gardeners interested in a natural approach.

I've divided these native plant communities into five broad groups: dunes and beaches; pine-oak woods; oak woods; beech-maple and hemlock-northern hardwood forests; and grasslands. I've left out wetlands because they present many special problems. If you have a natural source of water on your site, by all means incorporate it in your garden; your plant palette will be greatly enhanced.

Because the following communities are so broadly defined, you should explore natural areas near your garden for more precise clues about suitable plants. Another thing to keep in mind is that most of these plant communities occur in patches in a great mosaic, and there are overlapping types of communities that aren't mentioned.

Dunes and Beaches

Dunes and beaches are restricted to the immediate Atlantic coast. Because these areas are continually disturbed by storms,

---

DR. STEVEN CLEMANTS *is a botanist at the Brooklyn Botanic Garden who specializes in the flora of the New York metropolitan area. Chairman of the New York Flora Association, he is currently working on a flora of Brooklyn.*

PLANTS FOR A DUNE GARDEN

···

Trees and Shrubs

Post oak	*Quercus stellata*
Pitch pine	*Pinus rigida*
Beach plum	*Prunus maritima*
Sand rose	*Rosa rugosa*
Bearberry	*Arctostaphylos uva-ursi*
Bayberry	*Myrica pensylvanica*
Poison ivy	*Toxicodendron radicans*

Forbs

Prickly pear cactus	*Opuntia humifusa*
Beach heather	*Hudsonia tomentosa*
Seaside goldenrod	*Solidago sempervirens*
Seabeach sandwort	*Honkenya peploides*
Seaside spurge	*Chamaesyce polygonifolia*
Beach pea	*Lathyrus japonicus*

Grasses

Beachgrass	*Ammophila breviligulata*

---

high tides and offshore winds, few plant species can grow here.

Very few species grow on beaches, and those that do usually colonize the beach naturally. Consequently, it makes little sense to try to garden on a beach; instead, try to keep at least part of it off limits to off-road vehicles so beach species can establish themselves.

On dunes, however, there is more diversity and more opportunity for landscaping. There are usually no trees, but occasionally a stunted post oak or pitch pine. If you enjoy bonsailike, weathered trees, plant a few. They'll add height to the garden as well as a distinctive look. But your dune garden should be dominated by beachgrass or shrubs. Among the first plants to colonize dunes is beachgrass. On sheltered or older sites shrubs are common, especially sand rose, beach plum, bayberry and poison ivy. Most dunes are a patchwork of bare sand, beachgrass and shrubs. Consider using all three in your garden. One of the biggest problems with dunes is erosion, so it's a good idea *not* to have large areas of bare sand.

In many areas dunes and beaches are protected. To make major changes you'll need a permit. On the other hand, there may be little problem with adding species to a pre-existing community.

Pine-Oak Woodlands

The woodlands that develop on poor sandy soils are often dominated by pitch pine and a variety of oaks. If you live on the broad, flat, sandy coastal plains of eastern Long Island and southern New Jersey, pine-oak woodland was most likely the original plant community. Occasionally this kind of forest is found inland on glacial outwash and rocky outcrops.

The type of oak species and the ratio of oaks to pine vary by site. In some places the oaks are dominant; in others the pine is nearly the only tree present. In any case, pitch pine and oaks should be the framework of your garden. The choice of oak depends on what specific plant community was in your area and the type of garden you want to create. Scrub oak and dwarf chestnut oak are low growing and will provide a shrubby look. Scarlet oak, black oak and white oak are taller and will cast more shade, but this may restrict what forbs and grasses will grow. All the oaks take many years to reach maturity. If the site already has mature trees, you may want to keep them and start the oaks in the understory. I recommend using a few well spaced pitch pines and possibly a few species of oak.

Pine-oak woods usually have grassy openings with a variety of forbs and small shrubs. Consider creating a garden around such an opening, because you'll be able to dramatically increase your plant palette. As a backdrop, use pitch pines and some of the taller shrubs like mountain laurel, azalea, huckleberries and tall blueberries. In front, mingle shorter shrubs such as heathers, broom crowberry and the shorter blueberries with forbs such as orange grass, asters, goldenrods, blue-eyed grass and wild indigo.

With proper choices this kind of garden can be colorful year round. In the winter the green of the pine will contrast with the browns of some oaks which retain their dead leaves until spring. Wintergreen, sheep laurel and holly provide additional color. In spring many species blossom, including heathers (yellow flowers), blueberries (white or pink flowers) and pyxies (white flowers). The new growth on the pine together with their male flowers provide a bright green backdrop.

In summer in the pine-oak woods, the laurels produce copious pink flowers. Other blooming species include wild indigo (yellow flowers), lupine (purple flowers), goat's rue (yellow-white marked with purple) and butterfly weed (orange flowers). There isn't a great fall foliage display partly because the pine dominates this forest. However, you can plant other species for fall display, including sassafras for bright splashes of yellow and sumacs and heaths which turn a vibrant crimson. The fall is also a time for many forbs to bloom — the golden asters (yellow), asters (blue), goldenrods (yellow) and blazing stars (rose-purple). Other species set fruit, such as orange grass (orange fruit) and wintergreen (red fruit). Also consider using grasses for fall display, particularly little bluestem which becomes yellow-brown with hints of orange.

Keep in mind, though, that there are several potential problems with planting pine-oak vegetation in a garden setting. First, this plant community is strongly influenced by fire. The best examples burn at regular intervals of 10 to 30 years. Several species have become fire-dependant; some pitch pines, for instance, need fire to shed their seed. Fire also keeps weedy species from encroaching on the native species. Because controlled burning is illegal in many localities you'll have to weed diligently by hand. Second, the soils typical of this vegetation

PLANTS FOR AN OAK GARDEN

TREES

Red oak	*Quercus borealis*
White oak	*Quercus alba*
Black oak	*Quercus velutina*
Chestnut oak	*Quercus montana*
Pignut	*Carya glabra*
Shagbark	*Carya ovata*
Sweet pignut	*Carya ovalis*
White ash	*Fraxinus americana*
Red maple	*Acer rubrum*
Eastern hop hornbeam	*Ostrya virginiana*

SMALL TREES OR LARGE SHRUBS

Flowering dogwood	*Cornus florida*
Witch-hazel	*Hamamelis virginiana*
Shadbush	*Amelanchier arborea*
Choke cherry	*Prunus virginiana*

LOW SHRUBS

Maple-leaf viburnum	*Viburnum acerifolium*
Blueberries	*Vaccinium* spp.
Red raspberry	*Rubus idaeus*
Spicebush	*Lindera benzoin*

FORBS

Wild sarsaparilla	*Aralia nudicaulis*
False Solomon's seal	*Smilacina racemosa*
White goldenrod	*Solidago bicolor*
Hepatica	*Hepatica americana*
Bellwort	*Uvularia perfoliata*
Canada mayflower	*Maianthemum canadense*
Trilliums	*Trillium* spp.
Trout lilies	*Erythronium* spp.
Asters	*Aster* spp.
Goldenrod	*Solidago* spp.

GRAMINOIDS

Pennsylvania sedge	*Carex pensylvanica*

Blueberries of the pine-oak woods turn a vibrant crimson in fall. Autumn is also the time when asters, goldenrods and other wildflowers bloom.

Pyxies (*Pyxidanthera barbulata*) in the New Jersey pine barrens.

type are well drained and dry much of the year. Some species, such as swamp azalea, sheep laurel and blazing star, grow around streams and lakes and may be difficult to grow on higher ground where there is little water. If you had to give the garden constant and massive infusions of water, you'd be defeating the whole purpose of a natural garden. You'd do well to stick to the drier vegetation.

Oak Woods

Throughout the metropolitan area bedrock is close to the surface, forming cliffs, ridges and boulder piles. In these areas, as well as parts of the coastal plain, oak dominates the woodlands. American chestnut used to be codominant in much of the area, but the chestnut blight has reduced or eliminated this species. On dry, rocky ridgetops or in openings in the woods, grassy meadows or pine-oak forests may be present; in these situations the plant community may be identical to, or very close to, the grasslands mentioned below or pine-oak woods mentioned above. On slopes oak-hickory forests or chestnut-oak forests predominate. In protected areas maple-beech forests or hemlock forests are present (see below). In this section, I'll concentrate on the oak-hickory and chestnut oak forests.

Oak forests generally form on well drained, acid and often thin soils. They therefore do not support a rich and varied flora. But don't let that stop you. A number of handsome trees grow with the oaks, including hickories, white ash and eastern hop hornbeam. In the typical suburb you'll be working with an existing stand of oaks surrounded by lawn. In that case you can plant understory trees, shrubs and forbs. Shadbush makes a striking white display very early in spring, before any other shrub blooms. Flowering dogwoods are beautiful tall shrubs in these woodlands (look for strains resistant to dogwood anthracnose);

other tall shrubs or small trees include witch-hazel and choke cherry. A well spaced and well chosen understory can create a wonderful setting for low shrubs and forbs.

Forbs, especially spring wildflowers, tend to be sparse in these forests because of the acid soil. However, this scarcity makes the appearance of wildflowers all the more exciting. You can space your wildflowers like small jewels to be treasured individually or you can create solid splashes of color. Spring wildflowers in the oak woodlands are often white. They include false Solomon's seal (white), hepatica (white to lavender), bellwort (yellow) and Canada mayflower (white). If your soil is richer, try other species like trilliums and trout lilies. Although there will be some carryover from the spring and fall, there is little that will flower specifically in summer. Fall is peak time for flowers in an oak forest. Asters, goldenrods and other members of the daisy family start flowering in late summer and continue till November. Combined with fall foliage and fruiting shrubs, they provide an autumn display that lasts for months.

Canada sedge is the most common graminoid or grasslike plant in these forests. It forms a dense turf. Consider this species instead of grass in your lawn. It grows only about five inches high, so you won't waste half the summer mowing.

Normally in an oak woods there are pockets of richer, moister soil where a wider variety of plants can grow. These pockets are usually found near the base of a slope or in protected areas. Use rock outcrops or boulders to form small areas of richer plant diversity in your garden.

Beech-Maple and Hemlock-Northern Hardwood Forests

Although oak forests predominate throughout the metropolitan area, beech-maple and hemlock-northern hardwood forests are found on the lower slopes of ravines, on

An oak forest on Long Island. Fall foliage, fruiting shrubs and asters and other members of the daisy family provide an autumn display that lasts for months.

Bird's foot violet (*Viola pedata*), a good candidate for a pine-oak garden.

65

TREES

Sugar maple	*Acer saccharum*
Red maple	*Acer rubrum*
Beech	*Fagus grandifolia*
Hemlock	*Tsuga canadensis*
American elm	*Ulmus americana*
White ash	*Fraxinus americana*
Yellow birch	*Betula alleghaniensis*
Red oak	*Quercus borealis*
Basswood	*Tilia americana*
Poplars	*Populus* spp.
Birches	*Betula* spp.

SHRUBS

Flowering dogwood	*Cornus florida*
Alternate-leaved dogwood	*Cornus alternifolia*
Maple-leaf viburnum	*Viburnum acerifolium*
Hobblebush	*Viburnum lantanoides*
Striped maple	*Acer pensylvanica*
Witch-hazel	*Hamamelis virginiana*

FORBS

Lily	*Lilium philadelphicum*
Wild ginger	*Asarum canadense*
Purple trillium	*Trillium erectum*
Jack-in-the-pulpit	*Arisaema triphyllum*
White baneberry	*Actaea pachypoda*
Wild leek	*Allium tricoccum*
Bloodroot	*Sanguinaria canadensis*
Blue cohosh	*Caulophyllum thalictroides*
Partridgeberry	*Mitchella repens*
Wood sorrel	*Oxalis* spp.
Round-leaf violet	*Viola rotundifolia*
Indian cucumber root	*Medeola virginiana*
Star flower	*Trientalis borealis*
Foamflower	*Tiarella cordifolia*
Canada mayflower	*Maianthemum canadense*
Purple trillium	*Trillium erectum*
Hepatica	*Hepatica nobilis*
Trout lily	*Erythronium* spp.
Rue anemone	*Anemonella thalictroides*
Trillium	*Trillium* spp.
Dutchman's breeches	*Dicentra cucullaria*
Bellwort	*Uvularia* spp.

FERNS

Rock polypody	*Polypodium virginianum*
Christmas fern	*Polystichum acrostichoides*

cool, mid-elevation slopes and on moist, well drained sites along swamps. Farther north these forests dominate the landscape.

Beech-maple forests usually develop on acid soils. Sugar maple and beech are the dominant trees but basswood, American elm, white ash, yellow birch and red maple also occur. There are relatively few shrubs and herbs, but characteristic small trees and tall shrubs include American hornbeam, striped maple, witch-hazel, hobblebush and alternate-leaved dogwood. The forbs include blue cohosh, jack-in-the-pulpit, white baneberry, wild leek, wild ginger, false solomon's seal and bloodroot.

The hemlock-northern hardwood forests, like the beech-maple forests, have beech and sugar maple in the canopy. But several other trees may also be present, including hemlock, red maple, black cherry, white pine, yellow birch, black birch, red oak and basswood. The amount of hemlock can vary from nearly pure stands to as little as 20 percent. Few species grow beneath the dense evergreen canopy of a pure stand of hemlock. Among the few are partridgeberry, wood sorrel and round-leaved violet. Where there are fewer hemlocks the forest can have a wealth of forbs, including Indian cucumber root, Canada mayflower, star flower, bellwort, foamflower and purple trillium.

On sites that once had beech-maple or hemlock-northern hardwood forests but have since been cleared and then allowed to regrow, the forests that first appear, called successional forests, are dominated by poplars, red maple and birches. As these forests mature the slower-growing beeches, maples and hemlocks grow up and shade out the colonizing species.

Successional forests present a wealth of opportunities for your garden. In the spring before the trees have leafed out, the forest floor is often a carpet of pastels — the greens of new leaves and the many hues of spring flowers such as Canada mayflower (white), hepatica (white to lavender), trout lilies (yellow), rue anemone (white to pink), trillium (white or purple), dutchman's breeches (white) and bellworts (yellow). During summer you can enjoy the lush greens of ferns set against the bright orange of lilies and white of baneberry. In the fall these woods are a kaleidoscope of color — with the brilliant reds of maples, yellows of beeches and browns of oaks.

Grasslands

There are several native grasslands in the New York area, including the Hempstead plains grassland, maritime grasslands and rocky summit grasslands. The little bluestem is a dominant species in all of them.

Maritime grasslands are found on sandy coastal plains within reach of the ocean's salt spray. Although this community is dominated by grasses there are a few wildflowers. Among the notables are Atlantic golden aster, bushy rockrose, hoary frostweed, flat-top goldenrod, white-top aster and pussy's toes. Since maritime grasslands often mingle with dunes and pine-oak woods in the wild, consider creating a mosaic of these communities.

The Hempstead plains grassland once covered approximately 38,000 acres of southern Nassau County, Long Island, but has now dwindled to less than thirty. It was once dominated by the same grasses typical of the Midwestern tallgrass prairie, including big bluestem, little bluestem, Indian grass and switch grass. There was once a

wealth of wildflowers, including wild indigo, dwarf cinquefoil, goldenrods, butterfly weed, stargrass, violets and asters. A few trees were scattered in clumps on the plains.

Rocky summit grasslands are found in the oak forest on the most exposed rocky summits. They are dominated by little bluestem, poverty grass and a few other grasses. Only a few spring wildflowers are found, such as dittany, but there are many fall wildflowers, especially asters and goldenrods. This sort of grassland can make a pleasant counterpoint to an oak forest garden.

The major problem with all of the grasslands is that fire plays an important part in maintaining them. Without fire, exotic

---

PLANTS FOR GRASSLAND GARDENS

FORBS

Atlantic golden aster	*Pityopsis falcata*
Bushy rockrose	*Helianthemum dumosum*
Hoary frostweed	*Helianthemum propinquum*
Flat-top goldenrod	*Euthamia graminifolia*
White-top aster	*Aster paternus*
Pussy's toes	*Antennaria plantaginifolia*
Wild indigo	*Baptisia tinctoria*
Dwarf cinquefoil	*Potentilla canadensis*
Goldenrods	*Solidago* spp.
Butterfly weed	*Asclepias tuberosa*
Stargrass	*Hypoxis hirsuta*
Violets	*Viola* spp.
Asters	*Aster* spp.
Dittany	*Cunila origanoides*

GRASSES

Big bluestem	*Andropogon gerardii*
Little bluestem	*Schizachyrium scoparium*
Indian grass	*Sorghastrum nutans*
Switchgrass	*Panicum virgatum*
Poverty grass	*Danthonia spicata*

Butterfly weed contributes bright splashes of color to a grassland in East Patchogue, Long Island.

A closeup view of butterfly weed (*Asclepias tuberosa*).

FURTHER READING

Blumer, Karen. 1990. *Long Island Native Plants for Landscaping: A Source Book*. Growing Wild Publications, Brookhaven, New York.

Cain, S. A., M. Nelson, and W. McLean. 1937. *Andropogonetum Hemsteadi: A Long Island Grassland Vegetation Type*. Amer. Midland Naturalist 18: 334-350 (Hempstead plains grassland).

Forman, Richard T. T. ed. 1979. *Pine Barrens: Ecosystem and Landscape*. Academic Press, New York.

Harshberger, J. W. 1970. *The Vegetation of the New Jersey Pine-Barrens: An Ecological Investigation*. Dover Publications, Inc., New York.

Reschke, Carol. 1990. *Ecological Communities of New York State*. New York Natural Heritage Program.

species invade and trees and shrubs begin to sprout. If burning is illegal where you live, you'll need to physically remove unwanted plants or mow the grassland late in the year after the plants have shed their seeds.

Urban Gardens

Recreating a native plant community in the city is a challenge. But if you're persistent, this can be a very rewarding kind of garden.

The first problem is figuring out what the native plant community was. There's little information about the original plant life of most major cities. If that's the case, use your imagination. Use any one of the vegetation types mentioned in this article, but

Adapted from Amer. Geogr. Soc. Spec. Publ. 36, 1964

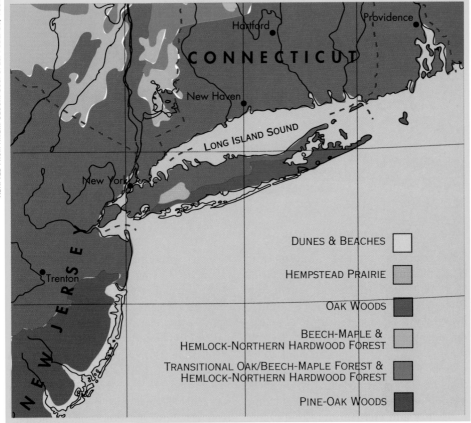

DUNES & BEACHES	
HEMPSTEAD PRAIRIE	
OAK WOODS	
BEECH-MAPLE & HEMLOCK-NORTHERN HARDWOOD FOREST	
TRANSITIONAL OAK/BEECH-MAPLE FOREST & HEMLOCK-NORTHERN HARDWOOD FOREST	
PINE-OAK WOODS	

NATIVE PLANT COMMUNITIES OF METROPOLITAN NEW YORK

make sure it matches the conditions in your garden, particularly soil and the amount of shade. If your garden is on sandy Rockaway or Coney Island, create a dune or maritime grassland community. If it's on a rock outcrop in the Bronx, a rocky summit grassland makes sense. If there are pre-existing trees, particularly native species, create a garden around them. Even if the species aren't native, keep them and plant small natives which will succeed the non-natives. If your garden is surrounded by tall buildings, plant understory trees and tall shrubs which are shade tolerant.

You'll have to experiment, and most likely you won't be able to fully recreate a native plant community, but you may be able to come close — and have fun trying.

Where to See Examples

You can explore native plant communities in parks, wildlife management areas and nature preserves such as those owned by The Nature Conservancy and the National Audubon Society. Many botanical gardens and arboreta have native plant sections which have been planted by the gardeners. These are proof positive of what you can accomplish in your garden. Some places to visit: Teatown Lake Reservation, Planting Fields Arboretum, Brooklyn Botanic Garden and The New York Botanical Garden. 🌐

NATURAL LANDSCAPES FOR SOUTH FLORIDA

BY GEORGIA TASKER

F rom its cypress swamps and pinelands to its sawgrass prairies and thousand-fingered mangrove fringe, South Florida's biological diversity was once legendary. The relentless development of recent decades has touched all of these areas, in some cases reducing them to ragged fragments. As wild areas have been so drastically reduced, growing numbers of gardeners, landscape designers and environmentalists have turned to the residential landscape as a means of restoring natural systems — if not entire plant communities, then substantial parts of them. Backyards are becoming repositories of habitat and hope.

Pinelands and Hammocks

In low, flat Florida, a ridge of rock juts up along the southeastern coast from Broward and Dade Counties to what is Everglades National Park at the tip of the peninsula. Pines that once grew loftily on this limestone outcropping did so with a particular group of fire-dependent plants that adapted to the rainy season's lightning strikes and the dry

GEORGIA TASKER *is the garden writer for the* Miami Herald *and author of* Wild Things: The Return of Native Plants.

season's withering heat. Seedlings of local slash pine develop a thick tuft of young needles, sometimes called a "grassy stage," and thick bark which insulates the cambium; the native coontie and the prostrate palmetto palm of the understory have subterranean stems from which new shoots emerge after fire prunes the old. The elevation and drainage of the limestone base of these pinelands — some reach five, ten or even fifteen feet above sea level — made them the logical places on which to build. Today, approximately one percent of this ecosystem remains outside Everglades National Park.

Five years ago, people said pine rockland habitat couldn't be restored. However, restoration specialist George Gann-Matzen, a third generation Floridian who has been recreating these pinelands, is now convinced that this ecosystem will be easier and less costly to restore in both backyards and on a larger scale.

Gann-Matzen has worked with Roger and Linda Blackburn to restore their former pineland. Located in suburban Miami, the Blackburns' sprawling single-story home was landscaped with exotic tropical plants around a few mature pines left behind by the developers. As the old pines began to decline, Roger Blackburn tried treating them with nutrient injections, but without much luck. Gann-Matzen suggested the Blackburns approach their yard as a whole system rather than one tree at a time.

Working with an overall plan by landscape designer Judith Evans Parker, Gann-Matzen began work in the front, where trees and undergrowth were cleared and needle duff removed to just an inch-thick covering. Gann-Matzen planted small pines, saw palmettos and beautyberries behind the arrival and entry court. Then, they waited.

The palmettos, freed of choking ferns, began to bud and develop new heads. Small pinelands herbs reappeared — ground cherry, pineland croton, coontie, gopher apple, three-seeded mercury. These species rapidly filled the open spaces, probably utilizing the leftover fertilizer in the topsoil. Now that initial spurt has stopped. Gann-Matzen believes that everything in the seed bank has come in, and the next step is to bring in additional plants to increase the diversity.

One difficulty in restoring a residential pineland is the need for periodic burning. When they caught fire naturally, the pines were kept free of invading hardwoods, and pine seeds germinated in ash-filled limestone pockets. Fire also nipped back shade-casting heads of the saw palmettos, creating sun-filled spaces for wildflowers and forbs such as white-topped sedge, wild petunias, blazing stars and rattleboxes. Burning now is a sensitive issue in residential neighborhoods. At the Blackburn residence, clearing has been done by hand. Gann-Matzen says that he'll keep cutting and hand pulling if he doesn't get permission to burn from the state and county. He anticipates he will get permission to at least use a propane torch. In any event, the Blackburn landscape is already the oldest pineland restoration done without fire, and Gann-Matzen is convinced that it works aesthetically and ecologically.

At the drive's edge and entrance to the Blackburn property, a group of exotic pongam trees has been allowed to remain, serving as nurse trees for the shade-loving juveniles of the hammocks. Hammocks are islands of hardwoods surrounded by different plant communities, usually pine or freshwater marsh. If pinelands are kept free of fire, they will gradually become hammock.

Behind the Blackburn's swimming pool, another hammock has been planted to screen the area from a neighboring two-story house. At the edge of the swimming pool, in planters that once held exotic birds of paradise and ferns, small trees and shrubs native to the Florida Keys now grow. The Keys plants are slower growing, and it is possible to look through them to the woods beyond. They include lignum vitae, *Guaiacum sanctum*, a prized tree that has sky blue flowers in early spring and wood that once was thought to produce a cure for syphilis; maidenbush, *Savia bahamensis*; *Guettarda scabra*, a tough plant called velvet seed; and the brittle thatch palm, *Thrinax morrisii*.

Another perimeter buffer has been created using shrubs of the pineland fringe: firebush (*Hamelia patens*) with tubular flowers that are magnets for butterflies; vivid green myrsine; white indigo berry, which produces ivory-skinned berries from which indigo dye is made; and spicewood, also called the pale-lid flower.

The cost of this kind of restoration is about $2,000 to $3,000 per one thousand square feet, depending on the size of the plants, the amount of labor required to remove exotics and the extent of the restoration.

Roger and Linda Blackburn have been willing to work at the maintenance of their acre in order to attain a high level of diversity. According to Gann-Matzen, gardeners interested in ecological restoration are so willing to get down on their hands and knees and work at it that it is possible to maintain extremely high levels of diversity. "We could maintain 200 to 300 taxa here

ABOVE: A picnic area nestled in Thelma Thomas's hammock garden. A bed of gamagrass (*Tripsacum floridanum*) was planted over the septic tank.

RIGHT: On a half-acre in Miami, a pineland was restored. A peach and aqua trellis and dwarf gamagrass lead the way to the door.

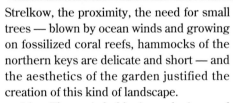

without a problem," he says. "Basically, that's equivalent to a ten-acre preserve."

A Hardwood Hammock Garden

Thelma Thompson, George Gann-Matzen's grandmother, lives on a 75x130 foot lot in Homestead, Florida, about thirty miles south of the Blackburn home. Mrs. Thomas's house is in a neighborhood of small, single family homes with yards that are open to the street and without a lot of fussy landscaping. Landscape architect Peter Strelkow, past president of the Dade County Chapter of the Florida Native Plant Society, designed a native garden that provides the woodsy feel Mrs. Thomas wanted. The garden is based on a Florida Keys plant community.

Homestead is within a few miles of Key Largo, the northernmost key. According to

Strelkow, the proximity, the need for small trees — blown by ocean winds and growing on fossilized coral reefs, hammocks of the northern keys are delicate and short — and the aesthetics of the garden justified the creation of this kind of landscape.

Mrs. Thomas's hobby is gardening, and she has an extensive bromeliad collection. Strelkow placed these plants so that she is able to see them from the house. Mrs. Thomas is also a butterfly lover, and the non-native pentas planted around windows unfailingly attract the native zebra butterflies with black and yellow striped wings and an occasional swallowtail as well.

All of the grass in the backyard was cleared, and three to four inches of mulch was brought in. Because the back was fenced, the clearing had to be done by hand. Most plants were three to five feet tall

when planted, although some trees were twelve to fourteen feet. Maintenance is simply a matter of weeding. Once established, the natives do not need fertilizer; the soil is naturally replenished by the humus created from the mulch and by falling leaves. Water is required only during long dry spells.

As is the case with natural hammocks, this tiny shaded forest is cooler in summer and warmer in winter than the area beyond its protective canopy. Among the trees used here are milkbark, *Drypetes diversifolia*, with whitish bark; paradise tree, *Simarouba glauca*, whose beautiful, shiny pinnate leaves are easily identifiable in the forest; pigeon plum, a source of food for white-crowned pigeons; crabwood, *Sapium lucida*, with the tiniest of notches on the leaf margins; Simpson stopper, with small, rounded leaves; and West Indian cherry.

This restored pineland in suburban Miami used to consist of exotic tropical plants beneath a few sickly pines left behind by the developers.

PLANTS FOR PINELAND AND HAMMOCK RESTORATION

PINELAND AREAS

Acalypha chamaedrifolia	Three-seeded mercury
Callicarpa americana	Beautyberry
Chamaesyce deltoidea subsp. *deltoidea*	Deltoid spurge
Chaptalia dentata	Pineland daisy
Cirsium horridulum	Purple thistle
Coccothrinax argentata	Silver thatch palm
Crossopetalum ilicifolium	Quailberry
Crotalaria pumila	Rattlebox
Crotolaria rotundifolia	Rattlebox
Croton linearis	Pineland croton
Dichromena floridensis	White topped sedge
Dyschoriste oblongifolia var. *angusta*	Twinflower
Erythrina herbacea	Coral bean
Eustachys petraea	Fingergrass
Flaveria linearis	Yellow top
Heliotropium polyphyllum	Pineland heliotrope
Heterotheca grandiflora	Silk grass
Jacquemontia curtissii	Pineland morning glory
Lantana involucrata	Pineland wild sage
Liatris laevigata	Blazing star
Licania michauxii	Gopher apple
Morinda royoc	Yellow root
Passiflora suberosa	Corky-stemmed passionflower
Physalis viscosa	Ground cherry
Pinus elliottii var. *densa*	South Florida slash pine
Piriqueta caroliniana	Piriqueta
Pteridium aquilinum	Bracken fern
Pteris longifolia var. *bahamensis*	Ladder brake
Quercus minima	Dwarf live oak
Quercus pumila	Running oak
Randia aculeata	White indigo berry
Rhus copallina var. *leucantha*	Southern sumac
Ruellia caroliniensis	Wild petunia
Sabal palmetto	Cabbage palm
Serenoa repens	Prostrate palmetto palm
Solidago chapmanii	Chapman's goldenrod

A Pineland in Miami

More recently, Strelkow reestablished a pineland in front of Raul and Irene Martinez's half-acre home in Miami. There were eight or nine existing pines soaring to nearly forty feet, but there was no understory, no mid-level or small pines — just a ground cover of exotic plants. When the weeds were removed, Strelkow found that a fair number of palmettos remained.

On the street side, Strelkow wanted to make an impact, so he planted bright purple queen (*Setcreasea pallida*) to contrast with the *Cassia chapmanii*, a native pineland shrub with yellow flowers. About fifty small and medium pines were planted, along with additional palmettos and beautyberry shrubs. In this garden, the pineland has paths through it. It is a bit manicured, not as wild as in nature.

Sorghastrum secundum	Lopsided Indian grass
Stillingia sylvatica	Queen's delight
Trichostema dichotomum	Blue curls
Tripsacum floridanum	Florida gamagrass
Zamia pumila	Coontie

HAMMOCK AREAS

Bursera simaruba	Gumbo-limbo
Calyptranthes pallens var. *pallens*	Spicewood
Cassia ligustrina	Privet cassia
Chiococca alba	Snowberry
Chrysobalanus icaco	Cocoplum
Chrysophyllum oliviforme	Satinleaf
Coccoloba diversifolia	Pigeon plum
Dipholis salicifolia	Willow bustic
Erythrina herbacea	Coral bean
Eugenia axillaris	White stopper
Ficus aurea	Strangler fig
Ficus citrifolia	Short-leaf fig
Galium hispidulum	Bedstraw
Ilex krugiana	Krug's holly
Mastichodendron foetidissimum	Mastic
Myrcianthes fragrans var. *simpsonii*	Simpson stopper
Myrica cerifera	Wax myrtle
Myrsine guianensis	Myrsine
Nectandra coriacea	Lancewood
Nephrolepis exaltata	Boston fern
Parthenocissus quinquefolia	Virginia creeper
Persea borbonia	Red bay
Polypodium polypodioides	Resurrection fern
Prunus myrtifolia	West Indian cherry
Psychotria nervosa	Shiny-leaf wild coffee
Psychotria sulzneri	Soft-leaf wild coffee
Quercus virginiana	Live oak
Randia aculeata	White indigo berry
Tillandsia fasciculata	Wild pine
Zamia pumila	Coontie

NOTE: The above list includes some of the species that have been or will be planted in the Blackburn garden in suburban Miami.

In the heavily planted front and side yards, restored pines are surrounded by bands of pineland shrubs and edged with colorful tropicals. To show visitors the way to the door, Strelkow designed a giant trellis in aqua and peach — a strikingly modern complement to this ancient landscape. He planted the vertical posts with a native pineland morning glory.

Experts admit that small restorations such as these will not duplicate nature, but they are hopeful that they can reestablish the look and feel of vanishing native vegetation, and include enough native species to sustain some of the local wildlife. "We obviously won't be able to save the big mammals, the deer and the Florida panthers and the bears," said Gann-Matzen. "But we can go a long way to saving the plants, the insects and the birds." ⊕

A backyard prairie in Lake Forest, Illinois, designed by the author.

PRAIRIE GARDENS

BY P. CLIFFORD MILLER

'm on my back in a sea of big bluestem, looking under the leaves of a milkweed for larvae of the monarch butterfly. Black-eyed susans, wild bergamot and yellow coneflowers surround me, colorfully framing the blue sky above. My three-year-old daughter sits on my chest, bemused by

---

P. CLIFFORD MILLER *owns a landscape design firm in Lake Forest, Illinois, specializing in the restoration and maintenance of natural areas. His work has appeared in* Garden Design *and* Architectural Digest.

the sight of her father lying prostrate on the prairie. A mallard spies us just before landing on the small pond nearby and veers sharply away, loudly voicing his disapproval of our presence. A song sparrow is chipping in the bur oaks nearby. I'm not in a nature preserve but rather in my own backyard, enjoying but a few of the many pleasures a prairie garden brings.

Whether your property is a 50-foot-wide city lot like mine or a 200-acre field, a prairie garden can be yours to enjoy as long as you have plenty of sunshine and a willingness to step off the well worn path of English and formal gardening.

The term prairie, from the old French word "praerie" meaning meadow, is loosely used to cover many ecosystems that are primarily dominated by grasses and forbs. Three hundred or more species may be present. In a prairie, woody plants take a back seat to the spectacular variety of native perennial grasses and herbaceous plants. There are mixed grass, palouse and coastal prairies as well as valley grasslands, desert grasslands and prairie savannas. In the central Midwest where I live, the tallgrass prairie used to dominate. However, only one-tenth of one percent of our original landscape remains, and only a fraction of that is virgin prairie. It is the tallgrass prairie and prairie savanna that I'll be referring to hereafter. But the same design principles can be applied to all prairie gardens.

Evaluating the Site

Whether you're creating a prairie from scratch or restoring a degraded one, the first step is a thorough site evaluation. You'll need to determine the type of soil you have, average moisture levels and availability of sun. Is the soil gravelly, sandy loam or predominantly clay? Perhaps you're fortunate enough to have one and a half feet of topsoil as the old tallgrass prairie did. If your site is on a rise where crops used to be grown, all or most of the topsoil may have long since eroded away. Digging a hole a couple of feet deep in various areas around the property can help you assess the condition of your soil. On too many sites I have found the original soil buried under a foot or more of clay backfilled around the house and compacted

In the front garden of the house on the opposite page, a sea of black-eyed susans in bloom.

77

with heavy machinery. This soil will be quite different from that on the undisturbed portions of your property. Map these different soil types on your site survey.

Include information on soil moisture as well. Is there a low spot that holds water for a day or two after rain? Do you have swales to channel the water off your site? Where does the rain water from your gutters go? I find it beneficial to put on a raincoat and spend time on the property during a storm. The bigger the storm the better. In fact, do this during several storms until you thoroughly understand water movement on your land. Low areas should be recorded on your plan as they may require a special type of planting. Many grasses and forbs require high levels of soil moisture to flourish — cord grass (*Spartina pectinata*), joe-pye weed (*Eupatorium maculatum*) and wild iris (*Iris virginica shrevei*), for example. In many conventional gardens, wet areas are problem areas that end up being drained or filled. I consider moist depressions an asset as they increase not only the plant species that you can use but the diversity of wildlife you will attract. For this reason I often create a depression if none exists. At my own house I partially blocked a drainage swale to create a home for moisture-loving plants. Be careful not to block up drainage too much or you may have an irate neighbor on your hands.

If you have no trees on your land, too little sunlight will not be a problem. But if trees do exist and you plan on leaving them, make sure you take into consideration the lower light conditions underneath them when you choose plants. Most prairie plants that tolerate some shade are also found in the savanna, a related plant community with scattered trees, particularly bur oaks (*Quercus macrocarpa*), magnificent trees with broad, spreading crowns, thick corky bark and leathery dark green leaves. The savanna would make an excellent ecological model for plantings under existing groves or scattered trees. Densely treed areas will require thinning or the use of a different ecological model such as woodland. Switch grass (*Panicum virgatum*) and wild ryes (*Elymus canadensis* and *E. virginicus*), shooting star (*Dodecatheon meadia*), smooth blue aster (*Aster laevis*) and golden alexander (*Zizia aurea*) are prairie and savanna plants that tolerate some shade. The north side of any structures, including fences, will also be subject to varying degrees of shade. Map these areas on your plan as well.

Next, inventory the existing plants on your property. Determine which, if any, will remain. If your site is an old meadow dominated by Eurasian weeds and grasses with just a few of the more aggressive native forbs like *Helianthus* or *Monarda* species, you'll be better off removing everything and starting anew. The same will probably be true if you're converting a section of bluegrass lawn to prairie.

Designing Your Grassland

Before proceeding any further you should consider other criteria — the size of the area you plan to work, how much time and money you have to devote to the project and whether the plants or seeds for the type of prairie you want are available. To choose the most appropriate plant community for your property, combine this information with the physical data on your site you've already put together. Obviously if you have a low, poorly drained site with heavy clay soils, it would not be a good idea to create a dry prairie usually found on gravelly knolls. If you're stubborn enough — and have plenty of money to spend — you can build a dry prairie on a wet site; it will just take many truckloads of gravel and bulldozers to move it all. It makes ecological sense to let your soil dictate, at least in part, what your final planting choice will be.

Existing vegetation is also a factor. For example, if a site has a few scattered ancient oaks but is dominated by old pasture plants predominantly alien in origin, I see the perfect spot for a savanna garden — I certainly wouldn't topple the oaks for a tallgrass prairie. On the other hand, if the site was in a secondary succession stage — say, an old pasture now dominated by pioneering woody species like cottonwood, ash and elm — I'd probably rip it all out and put in a moist prairie. One of the pitfalls of designing from an ecological community approach is that you tend to become something of a plant snob. Plants from "the wrong side of the tracks" (that is, alien) tend to be scorned, and often destroyed. Even some of the more aggressive natives start to show up on your unwanted list.

Obviously, it's important to have a good understanding of the prairie communities suitable for your area. If you don't, take the time to learn about them or hire someone who does know. Most of the better prairie seed or plant suppliers have lots of free information (see the list at the end of the article). If you can, get out and explore a natural prairie nearby. Note what it is you like about the prairie. Is it the broad sweep of grasses undulating in the breeze, the openness of the expanse or the myriad of flowers and continually shifting colors? Be sure to incorporate these features in your plans. Include your favorite prairie plants in the seed mix if they're appropriate for your site.

Planting Your Prairie

Preparing the site is the first step in the construction of a prairie. Removing all unwanted vegetation is the first task at hand. You can do this a couple of different ways. In small areas you can smother existing vegetation, for example a bluegrass lawn, by covering it with several layers of newspaper weighted down. Sheets of plastic or even old boards will work if left in place long enough. Removal of all roots and crowns and repeated tilling as weed seeds sprout is another alternative. If you are going to use potted or bare root plants, you're now ready to plant. If you're seeding, it would be a good idea to prepare a good seed bed by raking. I usually use three to five pounds of forb seed with four to five pounds of grass seed per acre. Others recommend up to 20 pounds per acre of forbs and no more than ten pounds of grasses. Due to the high cost of forb seed, I find this impractical. On small plots I may up my ratio of forbs to seeds a bit.

Spread the seed by hand, with a spreader or, on large areas, an agricultural seed drill modified for prairie seed. All of our smaller sites (under one acre) are done by hand or with a regular seed spreader. The spreader works best if you first mix the seed with slightly moist sand. This suspends the smallest seeds evenly with the largest ones, prevents them from dropping out early and ensures an even spread of the mix. The sand also lets you see where you have already seeded as you go along. Lightly rake the seed into the prepared bed and, if practical, mulch it. On a small area, grass clippings spread lightly will suffice. Do not water the garden unless you're in the midst of a drought. Water and fertilizer usually end up benefitting the annual weeds more than anything else. Do not use straw or hay unless it is weed and seed free, which is doubtful. Many are the seed beds mulched with straw I've seen which turned into old hayfields.

I highly recommend using a cover crop. Oats work well. They come up quickly, provide protection for the young prairie plants while also holding the soil in place and do not cast too much shade. Twenty to thirty pounds per acre should suffice. Canada wild rye used at the rate of five pounds per acre is a good longer-term cover crop that won't

Bright orange butterfly weed and violet-purple prairie clover against a canvas of green grasses in an Illinois garden.

persist like some of the perennial ryes will. Some people like to use perennial rye to increase the vegetative mass until the prairie becomes established. This allows you to burn the prairie sooner, providing more fuel for the fire.

Burning is the primary long-term maintenance tool for prairie gardeners. Fire was probably the single most important reason that prairies dominated so much of the Middle West. Whether set by lightning or Native Americans, these huge blazes roared across miles of land, causing little damage to the herbaceous species but killing all the woody plants. The line where forest met the prairie would undulate throughout the years as a direct result of the frequency of fire.

Prairie Maintenance

Prairies need remarkably little maintenance, especially once they are established. As mentioned above, don't fertilize or water the garden if you've seeded. If the oats come up well you know that enough moisture is present for the prairie plants. Plugs or bare-root plants will require watering the first year.

It is a good idea to mow your prairie garden two to four times the first year to prevent weedy annuals from choking out the smaller prairie plants. Do not cut any shorter than six inches high. Mow once in early June the second year and then, if everything goes well, you should be able to begin burning in the spring of the third or fourth year. In the meantime, you can remove weeds — very carefully — so you don't disrupt the prairie seedlings. And you want to disturb the soil as little as possible so the pesty annuals can't seed themselves in. Sometimes it's best to just leave it alone and give it time.

If you are unable to burn for safety, health or legal reasons, mow the prairie once a year in late fall or early spring. If you can burn, do it at least every two or three years. I prefer early spring, weather permitting, since that allows wildlife to use the prairie as cover and a food source through the winter. If the prairie is larger than one acre, I usually only burn half of it every other year so as not to disrupt wildlife too much.

Do not take a prairie fire lightly. Before burning, make sure you have plenty of water, wet brooms, rakes and other people to assist you. Protect any adjacent property with fire lanes. Bluegrass lawns or pathways, driveways, tilled earth, rivers or roads are all adequate firestops. Be sure to protect any nearby woody plants from the heat of the fire. If you're creating a savanna and have planted small trees, cut away any heavy duff accumulation from around the base of each tree and spot burn a ring at least ten feet across with the tree in the center. Older, larger trees native to savanna areas like bur oak and shagbark hickory (*Carya ovata*) are tolerant of fire and need no protection.

Once your prairie is established, occasional burning will be the only maintenance required. However, many things can and do go wrong during the establishment period. In certain areas the seed may not take well and you may have to reseed them. Remember, the prairie plants may take three years or more to become established, so give it time. Certain aggressive natives like prairie coreopsis (*Coreopsis tripteris*) and some *Solidago* and *Helianthus* species may take hold very fast and choke out less aggressive plants nearby. Removal and reseeding may be necessary. In my own prairie garden, now six years old, I've just completed a season of this type of control; it will be three more years before I know if I've been successful.

I've yet to come across an insect that I would consider a pest in my prairie, so I don't recommend the use of insecticides. Insects are an integral part of the prairie garden and usually coexist nicely with the plants. Some of the most beautiful creatures in my prairie are insects and it can be fun observing their habits.

My prairie garden is by far the richest and most diverse part of my yard. As small as it may be, it provides food and shelter for wildlife, a constantly changing palette of color, countless bouquets for the home and a source of great pleasure. Each time I wander through it I discover something new. Put native plants together to form an ecological community and amazing things can happen. Keep an eye out for your first monarch larva on the underside of a milkweed leaf. ⊕

SUPPLIERS

There are hundreds of prairie forbs and grasses. The following suppliers can provide you with extensive plant lists as well as the seeds and plants themselves. They're also excellent sources of advice on which species are most suitable for your site.

THE NATURAL GARDEN
38W443 Highway 64
St. Charles, IL 60175
Plants and seeds

COUNTRY ROAD GREENHOUSES, INC.
P.O. Box 62, RR 1
Malta, IL 60150
Plants

LaFAYETTE HOME NURSERY, INC.
LaFayette, IL 61449
Seeds

PRAIRIE NURSERY
P.O. Box 306
Westfield, WI 53964
Seeds and plants

PRAIRIE RIDGE NURSERY
R.R. 29738 Overland Road
Mt. Horeb, WI 53572
Seeds and plants

NORTHWIND NURSERY
P.O. Box 95
Springfield, WI 53176
Plants

A GARDEN FROM THE COAST OF CALIFORNIA

BY JUDITH LARNER LOWRY

Here on the coast of California thirty miles north of San Francisco, an enchanting array of plants from dune and bluff, chaparral and grassland is a magnet for tourists, botanists and wildlife. Yet most of the gardens in my little town are bereft of the native flora. In many of the vacant lots, invasive plants, some introduced by gardeners, have pushed out native plant communities and their associated insect, bird and mammal life, creating virtual biological deserts.

It's challenging to try to piece together a picture of what this area may have looked like before grazing, tree removal, suppression of fires and the invasion of exotic plants. For years I've roamed the surrounding Point Reyes National Seashore and Golden Gate National Recreation Area searching for clues. Oral histories in our local museum have provided the stray comment on the original plant life. "Wildflowers everywhere," said one. But which ones? Old photographs show mostly grasslands, but before grazing and firewood cutting, some said that the coast live oak (*Quercus agrifolia*) as well as

JUDITH LARNER LOWRY *is the proprietor of Larner Seeds, a mail-order seed company supplying California native plants and seeds to gardeners and the restoration industry.*

buckeyes (*Aesculus californica*) and coffeeberries (*Rhamnus californica*) were common. So an enjoyable, and ongoing, kind of detective work has produced the plant list for my California coastal garden.

My house is a quarter mile from the ocean in the town of Bolinas. The garden is a flat and rectangular quarter acre. It includes a coastal flower border ten feet wide and seventy-five feet long, and a section for coastal prairie plants. Plants from coastal prairie, chaparral and dune mingle in my garden — as many of them intergrade naturally in the wild as well. Initially the plants came from various native plant nurseries in the Bay Area. Recently, most of them have come from plants we've grown ourselves from locally collected seed. They also supply our mail-order seed company which specializes in California natives.

Chaparral and Prairie

The hills and plains around Bolinas are partially mantled with a scrub community known as coastal chaparral, which occurs in regions near the coast with mild, wet winters and dry summers. Chaparral is comprised of low-growing shrubs, herbaceous perennials and annuals. Plants typical of the adjacent dunes and inland scrub are sometimes intermixed. The plants of both the scrub and dunes are closely spaced, creating a dazzling tapestry of greens of subtly contrasting textures. Low-mounded plant forms predominate, kept compact and shapely by the sun and wind.

In the garden, I've used this mounding carpet of grays and greens as a model. I've grouped together some of the larger shrubs from the coastal chaparral, like coyote bush, to create keynotes and restful places for the eye. Growing nearby, and also in our garden, are a groundcover form, a medium-sized shrub and a treelike form. All provide rich medium-green foliage and a late-blooming flower that is one of the only sources of nectar for insects in the fall. Though many gardeners remove it from their gardens, coyote bush is indispensable habitat for insects and birds and small mammals and can be placed and pruned so as to tie the garden in with the surrounding native landscape.

Growing with coyote bush are the California sage and sticky monkeyflower. It's been said that you can't talk about California without talking about the sage, so evocative and typical are its soft silvery wands of foliage, its fragrance and its indescribable sage-green color. A hillside with a mosaic of coyote bush, monkeyflower and California sage rests an eye wearied from the drama of pounding surf and dazzling blue sky.

Though it is a plant from the southern coastal scrub, I couldn't resist introducing *Salvia leucophylla* to our north-central coast garden. Its lavender flower spikes are lovely, and so is its foliage, which is silver-gray and fragrant. It is a wide-spreading shrub, growing quickly into the tightly woven mosaic of grays and blue-greens that is characteristic of the coastal scrub.

On either side of the back gate resides *Solanum wallacei* from the Channel Islands, a leaning shrub with large purple flowers eight months of the year. A favorite of visitors to the garden, it has a somewhat disturbing tendency to spread by under-ground runners when it is content. These runners can easily be dug and given to admirers, but I would hesitate to introduce this plant into a natural area.

Although we like the garden bared to sun and wind to keep the coastal natives shapely, some areas require a more sheltered feeling, and it is here that we've introduced some of the taller coastal shrubs and small trees which, with their rounded forms and appropriate heights, have much to offer coastal gardeners. The Monterey pines and Monterey cypresses routinely planted in this area have proven a disaster. Although they grow to the size of forest trees, their root systems do not match their above-ground bulk, and they become an unwieldy hazard. They block ocean views, which used to be unimpeded, and significantly change the windswept, rounded contours of the original landscape. I've found the local palette of large shrubs and small trees to provide excellent windbreaks and almost year-round flowers, and to have little need for the tree surgeon. I like the local wild lilac from nearby Mt. Tamalpais with its fragrant sky-blue blossoms in early spring as a quick-growing windbreak and hedge. It reaches mature size quickly and lives for twenty years in the garden. Another favorite local hedge plant is coffeeberry, excellent for background plantings. Light-green new growth in the spring contrasts pleasantly with its mature dark-green leaves.

An excellent "nurse plant" and quick-growing windbreak is the tree mallow. This shrub has amazing recuperative power, recovering quickly from depredation by both gopher and deer. I view it as a decoy plant, since it receives the bulk of the onslaught of both these plant munchers in our garden but is usually able to recover. Growing to twelve feet tall, it has rosy-pink blossoms much of the year. Another suitable shrub is the showy island bush poppy, with yellow poppy-like flowers which contrast with its hand-

The author's coastal
flower border.

A creamy white form of
the native poppy.

Channel Islands
potato vine.

The coastal form of the
California poppy.

some blue-gray ovate leaves. This shrub prefers sun and good drainage and has surprised us with its quick growth. Equally vigorous is the red elderberry, a shrub with tropical-looking foliage, lush and rounded. Its creamy white blossoms in large heads are an added bonus.

In the coastal prairie section of the garden, I experiment with different combinations of grasses and wildflowers, most of which are no longer in evidence in this area — or so I originally thought. California fescue is one of the stars. I've found this fountainlike, wide-spreading, stately grass in many different environments, from a clearing in the mixed evergreen forest to a wind-blown coastal bluff, where it grew with lizard tail and coyote bush. We planted one-gallon containers two feet apart, based on our observations from nature. However, they spread, with the modest encouragement of our mulch, to at least three feet wide. This is a grass that you don't want to see crowded, as its form is too beautiful to lose. In a mature stand in nature, the spacing is perfect.

Pacific reedgrass is a majestic grass four feet tall and equally broad. Found in damp coastal forests and on moist dunes, it seems happy in our relatively dry garden. Handsome throughout the year, it makes an excellent specimen plant.

Another promising grass is coastal hairgrass, a low-growing bunchgrass with a pincushion form, particularly pleasing when its inflorescenses mingle with the leaf blades.

Native coastal chaparral — a dazzling, low-mounded tapestry of shrubs, herbaceous perennials and annuals kept compact and shapely by the wind.

It's a good idea to burn this grass every few years so that it retains its neat shape.

Coastal Perennials

Amidst this framework of shrubs or grasses are lower-growing perennials. One of the glories of our garden is the long-blooming coastal form of the California poppy, a small plant eight inches wide and five inches tall. I must say that it has become fairly aggressive away from its sand dune habitat. It's difficult, though, to complain about a plant with such exquisite blue-gray foliage and dazzling satiny yellow petals which blooms for five months — with no water. This plant's mounding habit as well as the color of its flowers contrast with the upright habit and crayon-orange blooms of the more commonly grown California poppy. There are seventy different strains of the California poppy in California; this is one of the worthiest.

Another dune plant that we grow both with the native bunchgrasses and in the flower border is the sea pink. A plant that has provided many cultivars to the garden trade, it has an elegance and grace that has sometimes been lost in the shorter-stemmed, darker pink garden forms. Rising on fifteen-inch stalks from a neat grassy mound, the ball-like pale pink flowers sway with the afternoon wind. Also a pretty addition to both grassland and flower border is the coastal wallflower. Technically a biennial, this low grower has cream-colored flowers with a pleasant fragrance. In our garden, bloom lasts for several months, beginning in early spring.

In late summer when many California gardeners are watering constantly to maintain any kind of bloom, one genus provides a wide range of pleasing pinks and whites and requires no supplemental irrigation. The eriogonums, or buckwheats, include two- to three-foot tall shrubs like St. Catherine's lace and Santa Cruz Island buckwheat. Recruited from the nearby rocky sandstone bluffs are the lower-growing eriogonums, like chalk buckwheat and its showier southern relative, rosy buckwheat. Butterflies are almost constant visitors to their pink and white flowers, held up from their silvery foliage on fifteen-inch stalks. Another butterfly favorite from the dunes is the beach aster, with a growth habit that combines well with the buckwheats and sea pinks. In August, its pale lavender, daisylike flowers are complemented by the orange-tapestried wings of the butterfly known as the West Coast Lady.

The Douglas iris is still another plant that moves happily from dune to bluff to grassland. More delicate in appearance than the bearded iris, our wild plant has a wide color range, from deep velvety purple to lavender to creamy white. Growing both in sun and part shade and in many different soils throughout the Coast Ranges of California, it spreads slowly through underground rhizomes. We use it in the windswept flower border and in the shade of an oak tree.

A Minimum of Maintenance

A native garden like this one requires little fanfare during planting and unbelievably little maintenance after that. Here on the coast fall or early winter, right before the rains start, is the best time to plant. Three or four months of weekly watering if natural rainfall is sparse is usually all that's required to establish coastal perennials when they're growing in their proper place. The rule of thumb used by most California gardeners — water even drought-tolerant natives through their first summer dry season — usually does not apply to these coastal natives planted along the foggy coast.

From the beginning, we've mulched heavily, with whatever materials we could find. We've never fertilized; the addition of mulch seems to create enough of a hospitable environment.

Our evolving natural garden has pro-

PLANTS FOR COASTAL CALIFORNIA

PERENNIALS

Armeria maritima	Sea pink
Camissonia cheiranthifolia	Beach evening primrose
Erigeron glaucus	Beach aster
Eriogonum arborescens	Santa Cruz Island buckwheat
Eriogonum giganteum	St. Catherine's lace
Eriogonum latifolium	Rosy buckwheat
Eriogonum grande rubescens	Rosy buckwheat
Eriophyllum staechadifolium	Lizard tail
Erysimum concinnum	Coastal wallflower
Eschscholzia californica var. *maritima*	Coastal California poppy
Fragaria chiloensis	Coastal strawberry
Iris douglasiana	Douglas iris
Lupinus variicolor	Lupine
Satureja douglasii	Yerba buena
Scrophularia californica	Bee plant
Sisyrinchium bellum	Blue-eyed grass

GRASSES

Calamagrostis nutkaensis	Pacific reedgrass
Deschampsia cespitosa ssp. *holciformis*	Coastal hairgrass
Festuca californica	California fescue

SHRUBS

Artemisia californica	California sage
Artemisia pycnocephala	Sand hill sage
Baccharis pilularis	Coyote bush
Ceanothus thyrsiflorus	Wild lilac
Dendromecon rigida ssp. *harfordii*	Island bush poppy
Lavatera assurgentiflora	Tree mallow
Mimulus aurantiacus	Sticky monkeyflower
Rhamnus californica	Coffeeberry
Ribes sanguineum	Flowering currant
Salvia brandegei	
Salvia leucophylla	Purple sage
Sambucus callicarpa	Red elderberry
Solanum wallacei	Channel Islands potato vine

duced plenty of surprises. Once we cleared the weedy exotics from the site, wild volunteers began to appear, including a native perennial lupine and the coastal strawberry. The lupine reseeds freely, and the strawberry has grown into a handsome ground cover. The native perennials I brought in have replanted themselves — one of the pluses of a garden designed and planted in accordance with local natural models. The coastal poppy, beach evening primrose, blue-eyed grass and the buckwheats have all reseeded vigorously.

From coastal chaparral to coastal prairie, you could hardly ask for an easier or more satisfying garden. It requires no supplemental water once established, no fertilizers or pesticides, just a bit of routine weeding. It is a garden to think about, to learn from and to connect you with that even more interesting garden that flourishes beyond the fence. ⊕

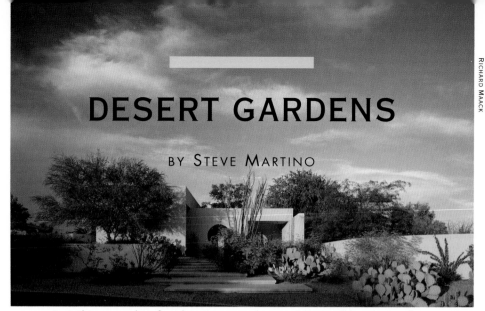

DESERT GARDENS

BY STEVE MARTINO

A striking garden for the Arizona desert designed by the author.

I grew up in Phoenix, in the heart of the Sonoran Desert, and I've stayed on to design gardens here. Phoenix, like most desert cities, has a deep sense of denial about its natural environment. When I first started designing landscapes in 1971, I used as much turf and exotic plants as anyone — that's what landscape architects did. The desert was viewed as a wasteland; anything you did to it was an improvement. As a child, however, nothing in the city had ever seemed as interesting as being out in the desert. This feeling resurfaced as landscape design became more and more of a passion. Ripping out desert natives and replacing them with alien plants that not only look out of place but need massive infusions of water and constant attention to stay alive came to seem shortsighted and foolish.

STEVE MARTINO, *ASLA, a pioneer in the use of native desert plants, specializes in landscape design and ecological restoration for arid regions, particularly Arizona and Texas. The designer of the John Rhuart Demonstration Garden at Tucson's Desert Botanical Gardens, he has received more than 60 design awards.*

I began to strive for gardens which evoke the special qualities of the desert. Appropriate plant selection, placement and massing, along with appropriate mulches and paveing materials, can quite poetically express the ecology of the desert and its sense of place. Using native plants was also the simplest way to make a home fit comfortably into the desert environment. As a bonus, desert natives are genetically suited to the soil and rainfall of the region, so water conservation follows. Creating functional and beautiful outdoor spaces that integrate human activity with the natural processes of a site — that's what my gardens are all about.

Wildness and Order

Site research forms the foundation for all my designs. I take soil samples and have them tested at Al Lengyel's agricultural lab in Phoenix. Our central Arizona soils are alkaline, high in salts, low in organic matter and microorganisms and usually riddled with layers of calcium carbonate or caliche that you either have to work around or jackhammer to make hospitable for plants. The water here is also alkaline and high in bicarbonates, compounding the problem. Organic matter must be added to soils with a high pH to give the plants the best possible start in their new environment. When I do a site analysis, I also look at the "big picture" — not just the site itself but also the streetscape, the neighborhood and the region. I tailor my designs to all of these to make the gardens feel at home.

In my designs I use the "hardscape" — paving, walls, fences — to structure and define space. I like the juxtaposition of these refined and ordered man-made elements with the wildness of an ever-changing natural garden. The right kind of mulch, or what I call "desert pavement," is crucial for a natural-looking landscape. Because rainfall is so sparse and plants must compete for water, the ground is not thickly carpeted with plants like the prairie or the eastern forests. Consequently, matching the rock types, sizes and colors of the surrounding landscape is important and requires an artistic eye.

Before I think about specific plants, I think in terms of plant forms or masses that will be needed to perform specific functions. What sculptural form or massing, for example, will provide privacy, a sense of enclosure and refuge? Where do I need to locate trees to cast cooling shade?

Exploring the Desert

When I first started using native desert plants, the landscape industry knew little about them. There was even less interest among gardeners and nurserymen. I was fortunate to meet Ron Gass early in my career. Ron is a naturalist, native plant specialist and nurseryman. I must have driven him crazy when I started hanging around his nursery. I would ask what seemed like a hundred times what each plant was. Most plants didn't have common names, and I could never remember the Latin nomenclature.

STEVE MARTINO

The Douglas garden in Mesa, Arizona, is inspired by the character of the desert wash, where plants are dense and lush. In flower is the chuparosa or hummingbird bush.

STEVE MARTINO

In the front of the border, pink penstemons bloom. At far right is the Sonoran Desert's most famous native plant, the saguaro cactus.

STEVE MARTINO

The author likes the bold, sculptural form of prickly pear cactus, at right. These plants also have spectacular flowers and need no supplemental water.

Ron and I became good friends and I traveled with him on several seed collecting expeditions throughout the Sonoran Desert. Several times we even ventured into northern Mexico. Ron had an intimate knowledge of desert plants. He knew the exact location and elevation where each of his nursery plants grew in the wild. He'd say something like, "I found this growing in Pepper Sauce Canyon north of Tucson in the Catalina Mountains." You can bet when I found myself hiking in that canyon ten years later, I was on the lookout for Arizona yellow bells. This kind of first-hand knowledge has made me a much more skillful and intuitive desert garden designer. However, until I developed some confidence in using these "unknown" plants, I'd show my designs to Ron and ask him what he thought about my plant combinations and whether he felt that they all fit together. Ron Gass's Mountain State wholesale nursery provided dozens of plants for my backyard designs in the early years. Today, he grows thousands of native plants for my large-scale desert restoration projects. Several of these species have no commercial market yet.

Desert Shapes and Shadow Patterns

I try to capture the character of the arroyo or desert "wash" in my garden designs. The wash is my favorite part of the desert. It's where the action is. These natural drainage ways are where the plants are dense and lush and animals come to seek shelter.

Whenever I saw a grouping of plants in nature that appealed to me I'd try to analyze what it was about them that I liked. I'd even photograph the scene for future reference. It was always the combination of texture, leaf pattern and color that made these combinations so remarkable. I especially like the effect of cactus growing out of plant masses.

Plants with bold shapes also play an integral role in my desert gardens. The relentless Arizona sun is a major element of desert gardening — in fact, I consider it an absolutely basic design tool. The blinding midday sun tends to flatten forms and colors. Only the strongest shapes remain distinct. The light doesn't soften and color doesn't return until late afternoon. The bold, distinctive shapes of spiked agaves (*Agave* spp.), ocotillo (*Fouquieria splendens*) and prickly pears (*Opuntia* spp.) hold their own against the brilliant midday light. They also cast wonderful shadows. Also basic to desert gardening is creating intricate shadow patterns on walls and paving — I'd go as far as to say that a tree's shadow is as important as the tree itself.

Penstemons and Prickly Pears

One of my favorite plants is the versatile mesquite tree. In fact, I use several different mesquites in either standard or multi-trunk forms — mostly the relatively small and slow-growing velvet mesquite (*Prosopis juliflora*) but also a new cultivar, *Prosopis alba* 'Colorado', developed by Mountain States nursery, which looks a lot like the popular Chilean mesquite but is more cold hardy, and the western honey mesquite (*Prosopis glandulosa* var. *torreyana*), which has the largest leaves and is the most open and airy tree. Mesquites grow from twenty to fifty feet tall, are handsome and extremely drought-tolerant and provide the most leaf area, and therefore shade, per gallon of water, according to studies by the University of Arizona. Their seed pods are a favorite food for many rock and antelope squirrels, as well as javelina. Blue palo verde (*Cercidium floridum*) is another favorite tree. This spiny deciduous tree, which grows fifteen to thirty feet high and wide, has distinctive blue-green bark and leaves and very showy yellow flowers in spring. I also like the sculptural form of prickly pear cactus, especially when contrasted with soft spreading ground covers. These plants have wonderful flowers and require no supplemental water. I most often use the native *Opuntia engelmannii*, which has yellow, pink and red flowers, the non-native *Opuntia ficus-indica*, an upright thornless tree-forming cactus with yellow flowers and big pads (leaves) and *Opuntia violacea*, which has red-violet pads and brilliant yellow flowers.

Arizona has the greatest representation of hummingbird species in the United States, and we also have the plants to attract them. My favorites, the penstemons, are even pollinated by hummingbirds. I typically use the hot pink *Penstemon parryi,* which produces an incredible show during March and April with its multiple three-foot-high flower spikes. I also use the orange-flowered *P. superbus*, the deep red *P. eatonii* and the lavender-blue *P. spectabilis.*

The chuparosa or hummingbird bush (*Justicia californica*) with its bright red flowers, the brittle-bush (*Encelia farinosa*) with its brilliant yellow blossoms and the strongly scented, olive green creosote bush (*Larrea tridentata*) form the basis of the simple plant palettes typical of my gardens. Other favorites are the ocotillo, staghorn cactus (*Opuntia acanthocarpa*), jojoba (*Simmondsia chinensis*), wolfberry (*Lycium fremontii*), indigo bush (*Dalea bicolor* var. *argyraea*), *Viguiera deltoidea*, native verbenas *Verbena goodingii* and *V. pulchella* and desert marigold (*Baileya multiradiata*), along with *Salvia coccinea* and *Salvia greggii* from the nearby Chihuahuan Desert.

Soil conditions dictate suitable species for a particular site. I always try to match the plants to the particular soil types in which they occur naturally in the wild. Except for the cacti, virtually all the plants need supplemental water until they become established.

Year-Round Color

One of the glories of desert gardening is that it's relatively easy to design a planting that will provide vibrant color the year-round.

Cliff and Marilyn Douglas's garden is a good example. At the Douglas garden, I had the opportunity to work on a site that was undisturbed, except for a faint jeep trail. We located the house on the only bare area on the five-acre site, thus preserving the rest as natural desert. The jeep trail became the driveway, and utilities were buried underground along this alignment. The Douglas house has washes on three sides, and the garden takes its inspiration from them. Although construction damage was confined to a small area, the small wash at the front of the house was totally destroyed. Brittle-bush, chuparosa, creosote bush and bursage (*Ambrosia deltoidea*) formed the basis of the site restoration.

Today, there's always something blooming. The real show starts in February with the chuparosa and its hundreds of red-orange flowers. Then the brittle-bush begins to bloom bright yellow. The penstemons and lavender verbenas bloom in March and April, followed by the palo verde trees with their spectacular yellow blossoms. In April, Arizona yellow bells (*Tecoma stans*) and desert willows (*Chilopsis linearis*) start to flower, and continue till November. The saguaro (*Carnegiea gigantea*), the Sonoran Desert's most famous plant, and other cacti flower through July. During the summer, their fruit ripens and turns deep red. The salvias bloom throughout the year.

When I began designing desert gardens, I simply wanted my projects to visually fit in with the environment, to look as if they belonged here. As my projects began to mature, an interesting thing happened. Wildlife would find their way to them and make themselves at home. First it was the pollinators, then the predators, then their predators and so on. I had unintentionally tapped into the food chain and was creating wildlife habitats — to the universal delight of my clients. These clients would be inspired to go on to learn more about desert ecology and become proponents for its preservation.

My garden designs make no apologies for the desert but rather pay homage to it and enhance it. A friend told me the story of how he once asked a Papago elder how he survived in the desert. His response was, "We do not survive here, we live here. This is our home." Desert gardening celebrates this spectacular environment and makes it a home for humans as well as wildlife. It doesn't try to turn it into something else. ⊕

Creating intricate shadow patterns on walls and paving is a basic part of gardening in the sun-drenched Desert Southwest.
ABOVE: the real squiggly, multistemmed ocotillo and its shadow.

WHERE TO GET NATIVE PLANTS

FIVE COMMANDMENTS FOR CONSERVATION-MINDED GARDENERS

BY JANET MARINELLI

Natural areas aren't just threatened by development, pollution and invasion by exotic species. To make matters worse, many are imperiled by private and commercial plant collectors who dig up native species from the wild. This isn't an isolated problem. Cactus rustlers in the Sonoran Desert threaten the saguaro (*Carnegiea gigantea*). Illegal digging is decimating wild populations of Venus's flytrap (*Dionaea muscipula*), the insectivorous plant found in boggy areas of the Carolinas. Orchids of the eastern deciduous forests, such as the white fringeless orchid (*Platanthera integrilabia*), are threatened by overcollection. Part of the problem is that plants like the native orchids are difficult to propagate. But because in most areas the nursery

JANET MARINELLI *edits BBG's* Plants & Gardens *handbooks and is the author of* The Naturally Elegant Home, *which will be published by Little, Brown in September.*

trade has not yet caught up with the upsurge of interest in natural landscaping, gardeners should be cautious when buying any native plant.

So what is the best way to acquire plants for your natural landscape? Here are five "commandments" to guide native gardeners:

I

 THOU SHALT NOT take a plant from the wild. It may be tempting to rationalize that taking "just this one plant" couldn't possibly make a difference. But it's almost never just one gardener or one plant. The cumulative impact of many trowels can be considerable. There is one exception to this rule — rescuing plants that would otherwise face certain obliteration by a shopping mall, suburban subdivision or other development. Collecting small amounts of seed to germinate yourself generally does not endanger healthy plant populations.

THOU SHALT make a point of educating yourself about the propagation and cultivation requirements of the native plants you're thinking of putting in your garden. Too many of the native species sold at garden centers and by mail-order suppliers have been dug up from the wild. Plants that are difficult to propagate or slow to flower or reach marketable size are the most likely to have been collected from their native habitat and therefore most at risk. Trilliums, which typically take five years or more to go from seed to flower, are the classic examples. Until nursery production of such species becomes profitable, don't buy them. Admire them in the wild instead.

THOU SHALT design your garden using only species that are easily propagated. Plants like rudbeckias and cardinal flower (*Lobelia cardinalis*) which are easy to propagate and quick to mature have most likely been propagated commercially.

THOU SHALT buy native species only from sources who state explicitly that their plants are nursery propagated. If they don't volunteer the information, ask. Don't be misled by ambiguous phrases like "nursery grown" or "field grown," which may mean that the plant was dug from the wild and grown at the nursery for a day or a week. The words to look for are nursery propagated. Your persistence will pay off: Nursery-propagated plants are generally healthier and better looking than those taken from the wild.

THOU SHALT make every attempt to use plants propagated from wild populations growing within 50 miles of your garden. Botanists are also concerned that the genetic integrity of local plant communities is compromised by the introduction of the same species from other regions. While local plants have adapted for thousands of years to the precise conditions of your area, plants of the same species from other areas have no doubt adapted to different conditions. Not just genetic integrity is at stake: Non-local plants may not perform as well in your garden as true natives.

The following organizations can provide you with helpful lists of nurseries selling propagated native plants: New England Wildflower Society, Garden in the Woods, 180 Hemenway Road, Framingham, MA 01701-2699, (617) 237-4924, publishes a regularly updated booklet called *Sources of Propagated Native Plants and Wildflowers* which includes species native to zones 4, 5 and 6. For a list of nurseries offering propagated Southeastern natives, send a stamped, self-addressed envelope to the North Carolina Botanic Garden, UNC-CH, CB 3375 Totten Center, Chapel Hill, NC 27599-3375. A list of nurseries in the West is available from the Native Plant Society of New Mexico, P.O. Box 5917, Santa Fe, NM 87502. It's also worth checking with the native plant society in your own state as well as botanical gardens in your area. ⊕

⊕ ■ INDEX ⊕

MICHAEL ANISFELD

A wooden bench invites strollers to sit and enjoy a bur oak savanna designed by P. Clifford Miller.